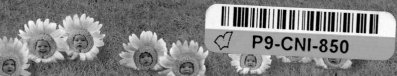

Anne Geddes

Down in the Garden

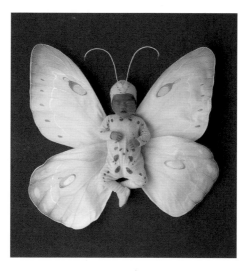

Andrews McMeel
Publishing

Kansas City

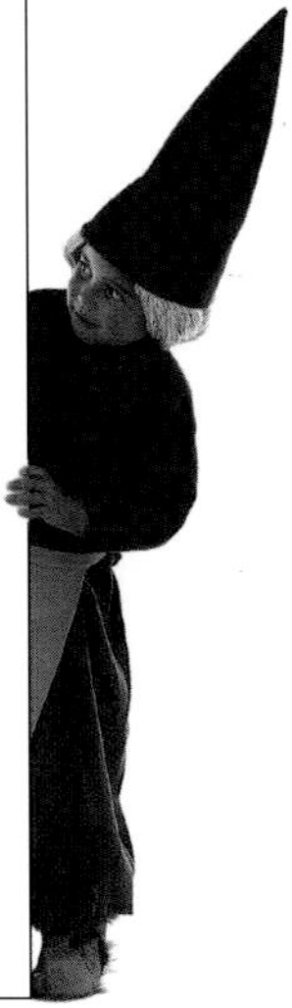

ANNE GEDDES ®

www.annegeddes.com

© 1996 Anne Geddes

First published in large format by Hodder Moa Beckett in 1996

The right of Anne Geddes to be identified as the Author
of the Work has been asserted by her in accordance with the
Copyright, Designs and Patents Act 1988.

This edition published in 2003 by Photogenique Publishers
(a division of Hodder Moa Beckett)
4 Whetu Place, Mairangi Bay
Auckland, New Zealand

Published in North America in 2003
by Andrews McMeel Publishing
4520 Main Street, Kansas City, MO 64111-7701

Produced by Kel Geddes
Printed in China by Midas Printing Limited, Hong Kong

ISBN 0-7407-3540-3

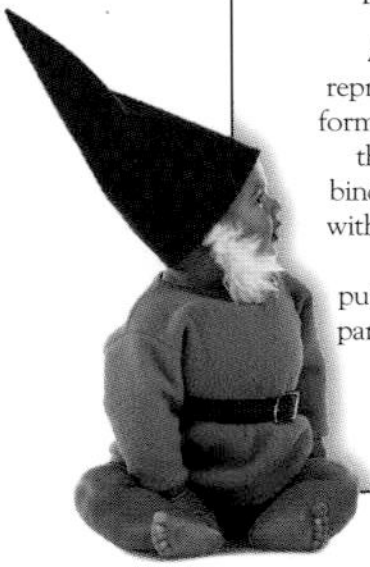

So many little babies and small children (the youngest only a couple of days old) have helped this book to become a reality over the past two years. You have all effortlessly made my ladybugs, bumblebees, hedgehogs, earthworms and various other garden inhabitants come to life with your own special charm. Thank you to every *gorgeous* one of you.

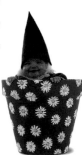

Thank you...

This book has been produced with the help of many people and although it is impossible to mention every one of them here, they know who they are and I am very grateful indeed to them all. The team who work with me deserve special thanks, as this has been an enormous project to take on. They have all been positive about each new challenge, no matter how much work it involved.

Natalie Torrens (my Studio Manager) has been invaluable behind the scenes in organizing babies and helping during the shoots, along with my assistant Emma Gee. Dawn McGowan has again worked magic with her wonderful sets and costumes, and every time I asked for more help she was there, ready and willing. Relda Gilbert (our film and technical expert) has coordinated the whole project. Jane Seabrook (our designer) has "lived" this book, as she said, for the past six months – thank you Jane for your unique input, and your wonderful watercolors, including the underground section of "Peggy's Worm Farm." The other members of the team, Rebecca Swan (black and white printing), Andrea Pickett (Office Manager), and Megan Daggar (Production Assistant), have all in their own special ways played an invaluable part in getting this book to print.

Thank you to Terry McGrath for his friendship, financial expertise and positive commitment to all of our projects, and to Geoff Blackwell from Hodder Moa Beckett, for just letting us get on with it, and trusting our judgement.

Thanks are also due to the team at Image Centre (color separations), Image Design (typesetting), Graeme Smallfield (compilation of flower images), Giselher Hagen (backgrounds), Gary Hunt, Jeff and Cecilia Kai-Fong, Mike Dowdall (San Francisco), Vicky Smuthers (San Francisco), Alistair Boot, Ron Simmonds, Lou Thackray, Glenis Foster (for her beautiful fairy costumes), Carol Rogers (teddy bear costumes), Zita and Bob Allinson, Ivan Crowther, and Jennifer Cook. The flower pots were painted by: Bev Goodwin, Grant Whibley, Sarah Cundy, Kirin Brock, Miriam Harris, Rebecca Gill and Anna Carlton. Both Anne and Natalie are also very grateful to midwives Cindy Haliburton, Ruth Davidson, and Rosemary Trethowen, and to the Twin Clubs of Central, Northshore, Southern and West Auckland for their kind assistance with locating babies.

The serious gardening advice contained within these pages was conceived via the collective horticultural wisdom of: Anne Geddes, Kel Geddes, Kirsten Warner, Natalie Torrens, Jane Seabrook, Relda Gilbert and various other "visiting experts." Reader discretion is advised! And last (but most importantly) for Kel, my constant source of encouragement, love and support; a wonderful sounding board for ideas, who also believes in fairies, and has shared my vision for this project from the very beginning – you always said my time would come…thank you so much for everything.

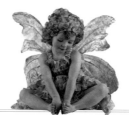

For Kel, Stephanie & Kelly,

and

Trena & Renée

as always...

Over the past two years, the fact that I have been endeavoring to produce a "gardening" book has been a constant source of amusement to my family and friends, who know how I truly feel about toiling in the garden, and didn't think I would be bold enough to admit it here.

However, I know the sort of person I am. I do not wish to spend hours in the garden working. But I can happily spend hours in the garden imagining what else could be happening there; hence the idea for this book, which originally came from my love of beautiful flowers and, of course, little humans! It is not as if I cannot appreciate the merits of a well loved and tended garden (indeed I wish I had one of my own), but I have no desire to get out there and tend it myself!

During the production of this book, I have been fortunate enough to meet many dedicated garden-lovers, who have been very generous with their time, advice, anecdotes and flowers! In particular, I would like to thank Rhys and Mrs. Jones (expert giant pumpkin growers, among other impressive gardening achievements), who were always there for us when we called, and who provided quite a number of items from their wonderful garden for this book, and the odd cup of tea as well!

If I were to single out any of the images produced in this book, I would have to say that "Peggy's Worm Farm" has been the most memorable. Over a period of six months, 55 little newborn babies came into the studio, and I photographed them all individually in their costumes (from my vantage point in the ceiling!) Once word got out, people were calling from everywhere with new babies, and there wasn't one baby who came in that we didn't include in the final image – in fact a lot of them slept through their entire visit to the studio. My only disappointment was that nobody managed to yawn during their photo session. I wanted just one "yawning worm!"

A lot of the little African–American bumblebees and ladybugs who are scattered throughout these pages were photographed in a studio in San Francisco (along with some of the bears from the "Teddy Bears' Picnic," a daffodil, and a number of the lawn daisies) as I wanted this book to be truly multicultural, and I have difficulty here in New Zealand finding babies of many different nationalities.

I am frequently asked why I photograph babies so often, and where my ideas come from. Little babies are indeed my inspiration, and I cannot imagine a photographic life without them playing a major part in it. Where this special love for babies comes from I cannot tell you, and I have spent much time searching for an answer myself. All I know is that they are all perfect little human beings in their own ways, and we should all take the time to cherish them, especially while they are very small.

I hope that, through my work as a photographer, I have been able to pass on my appreciation of the beauty and charm of little children. As adults, we all need to stop occasionally and look at ourselves and our circumstances with an open mind and a sense of humor, and remember to appreciate the simple things in life, which are often the most important.

In an indirect way, this book is a tribute to the role of mothers. Most mothers truly are extraordinary. They do a wonderful job under sometimes the most stressful of circumstances, and with little professional acknowledgement from the wider community. I recently read a wonderful quote in a magazine article which says, "The decision to have a child is to accept that your heart will forever walk around outside of your body."*1 I deal with many mothers on a daily basis in the studio and you all deserve as much encouragement as possible, because you are so special. A wonderful lady called Peggy Fleming, who used to be our next door neighbor, told our oldest daughter (who was two years old at the time) that when it rained the fairies all came out on the leaves with their little towels to shower, because that was the only opportunity they had to bathe. If you look out of your window next time it rains, you will surely see them all if you look closely enough, and with the eyes of a child. Children are the true believers, and some of us are lucky enough to make the transition to adulthood without ever losing the ability to see through young eyes.

While I was writing this book, someone said that they had read that fairies communicate with little babies all the time. What a wonderful concept! If you don't believe in fairies, you probably won't believe a lot of what you see in this book, but then it wasn't produced for someone who isn't a believer in things magical.

This book is pure fantasy. No matter how old you are, I hope that you enjoy your journey through the pages even half as much as I have enjoyed creating it, that you don't take any of my gardening advice too seriously, and that afterwards you will have the wonderful ability to look at gardens (and life!) in a whole new light. Most of all, have fun!

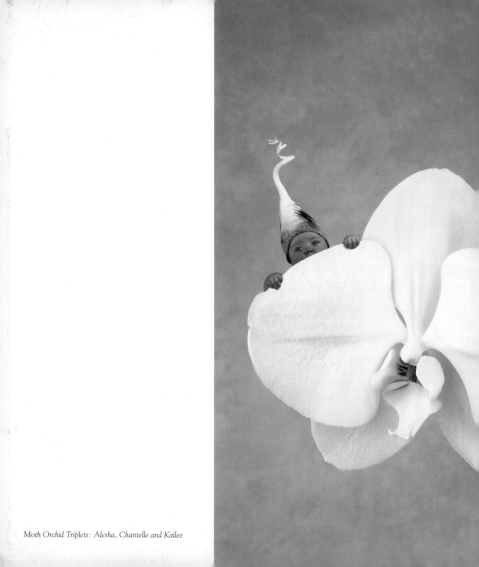

Moth Orchid Triplets: Alesha, Chantelle and Kailee

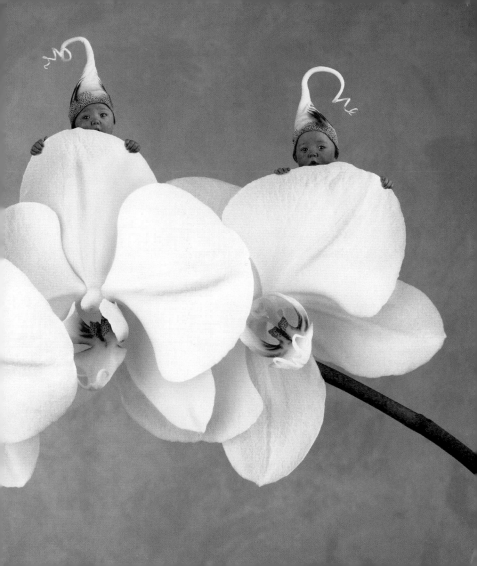

There's no

rushing

a garden…

…everything

grows at its

own p a c e.

Julia Snail

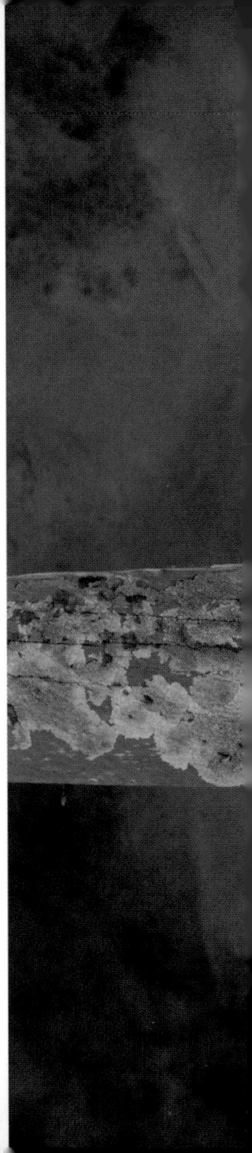

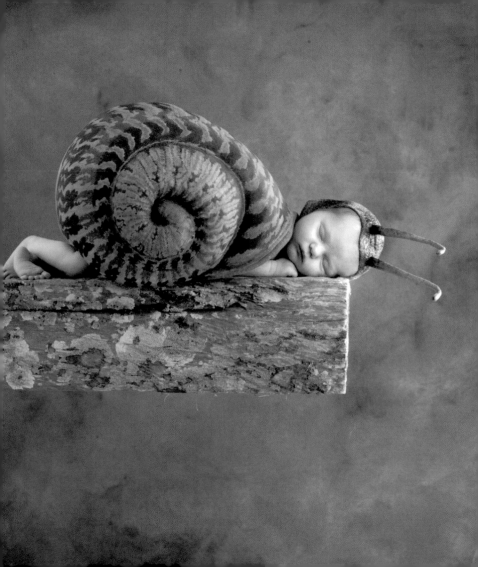

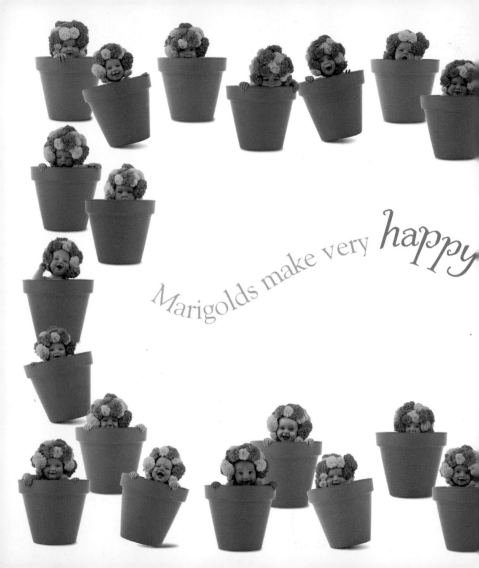

Marigolds make very *happy*

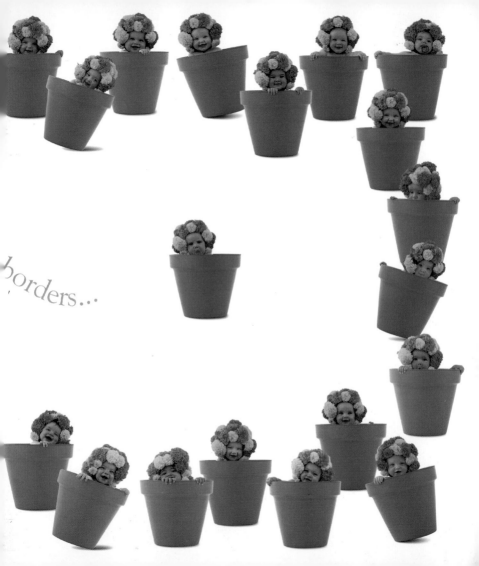

borders...

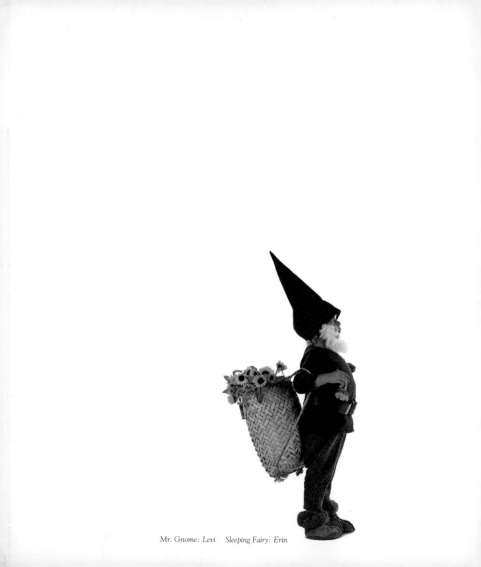

Mr. Gnome: Levi   Sleeping Fairy: Erin

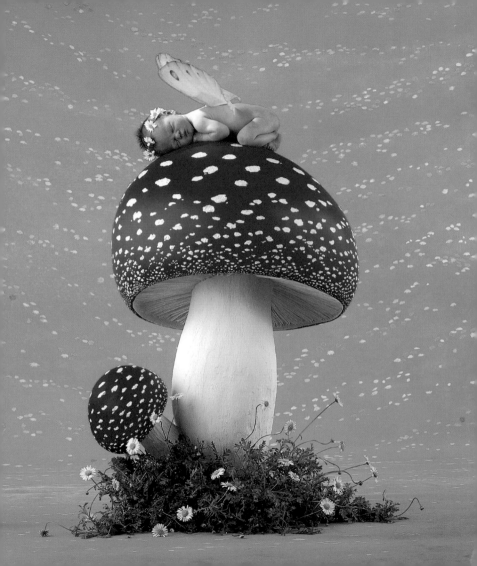

The

OLDER

boots get,

the more

c o m f o r t a b l e

they

become.

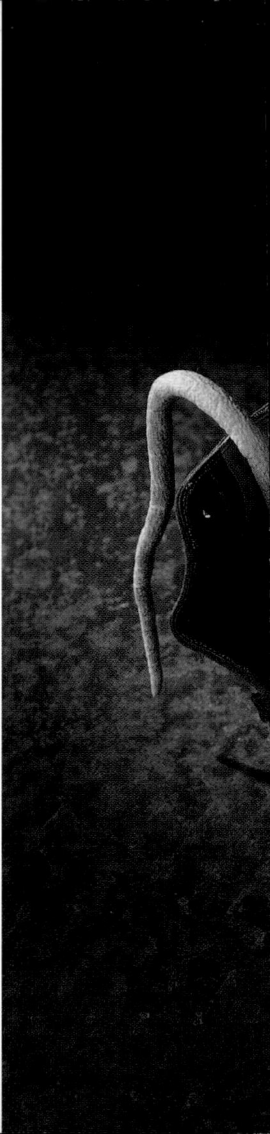

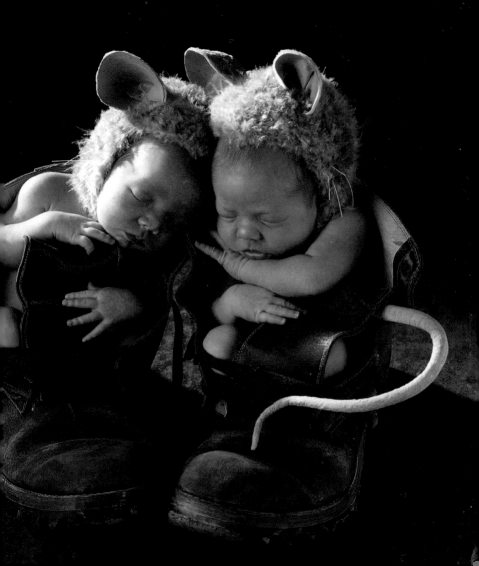

You

are

what

you

eat…

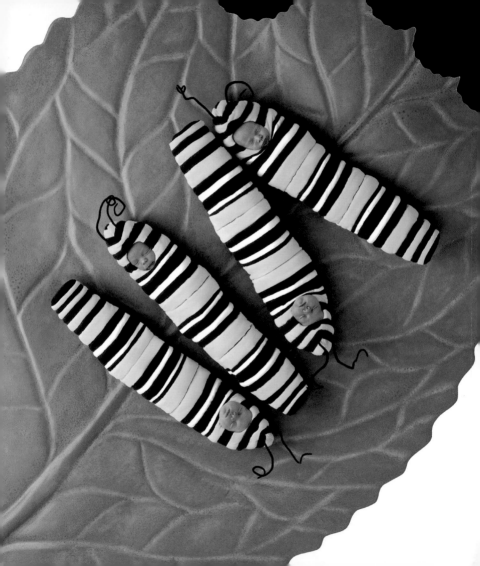

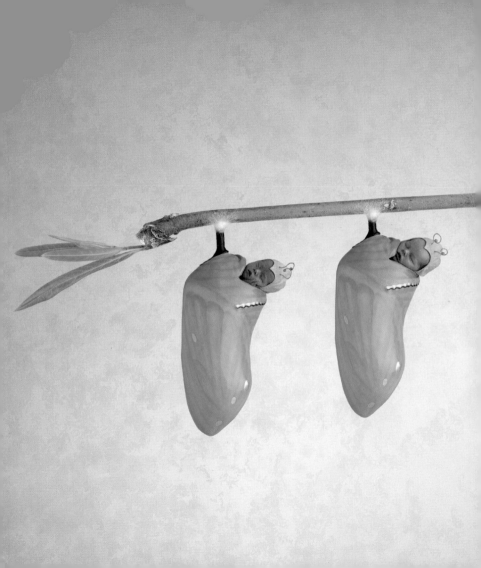

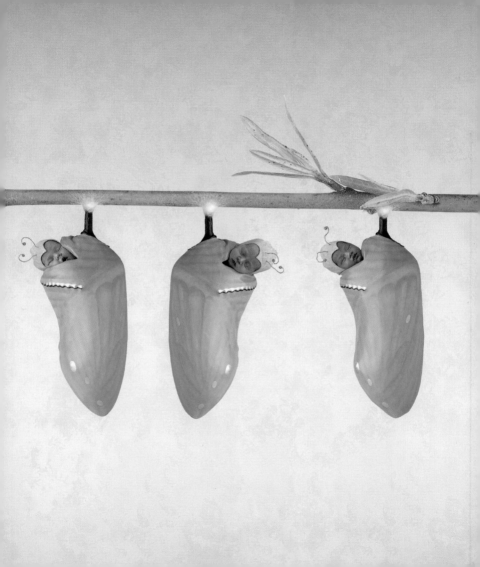

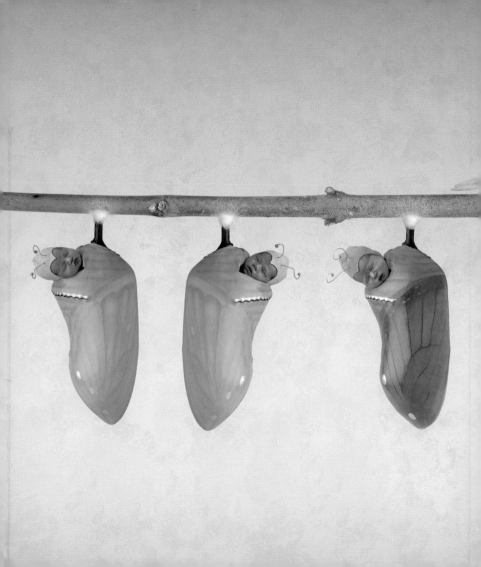

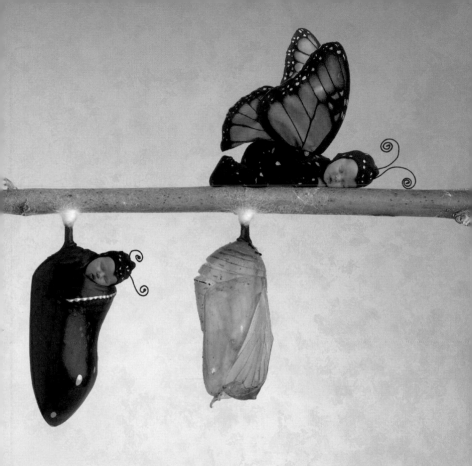

All good things take time......

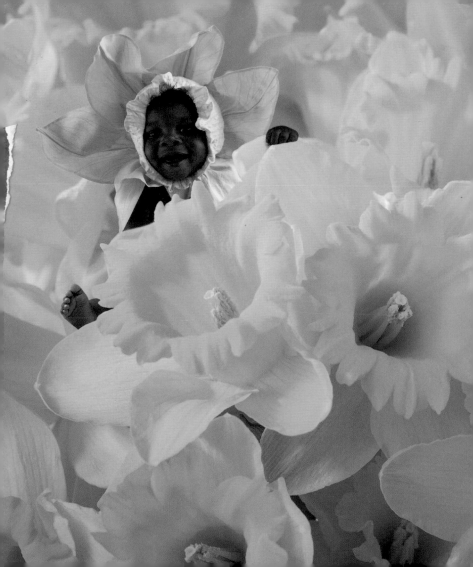

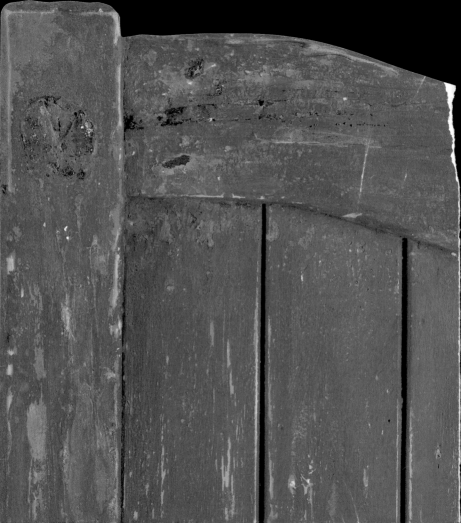

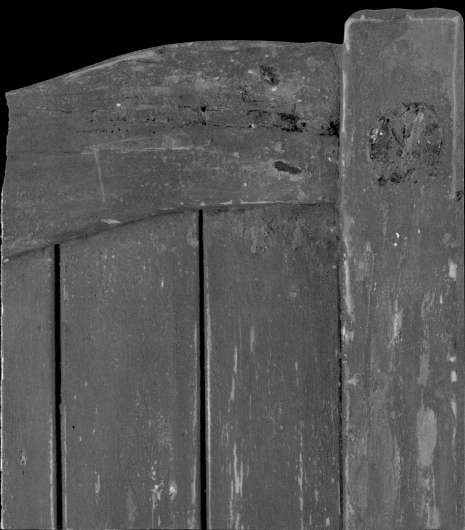

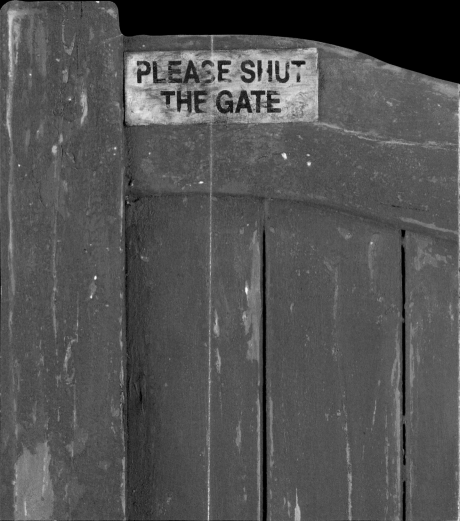

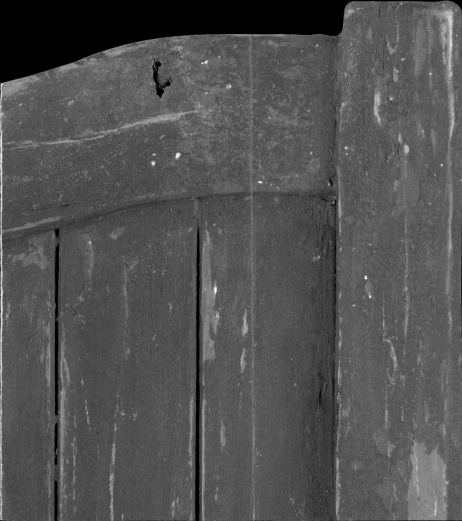

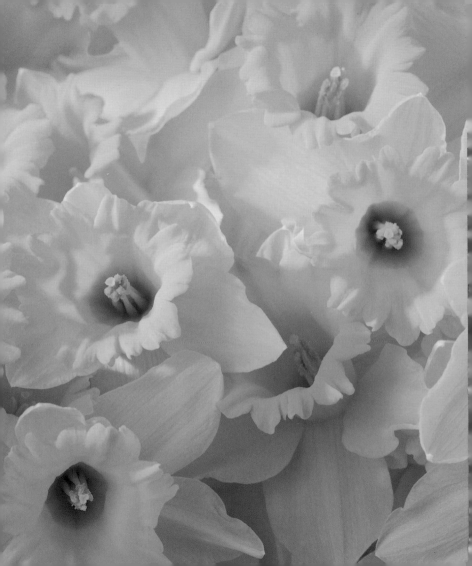

Are you

s u r e

they're

aphids

on your

r o s e s ?

Aphids: Callum and Sam

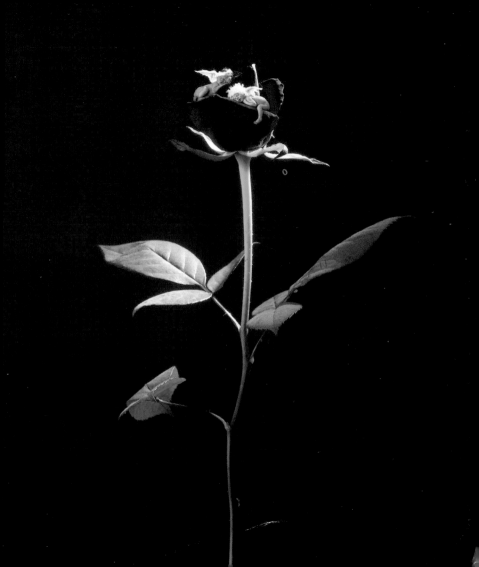

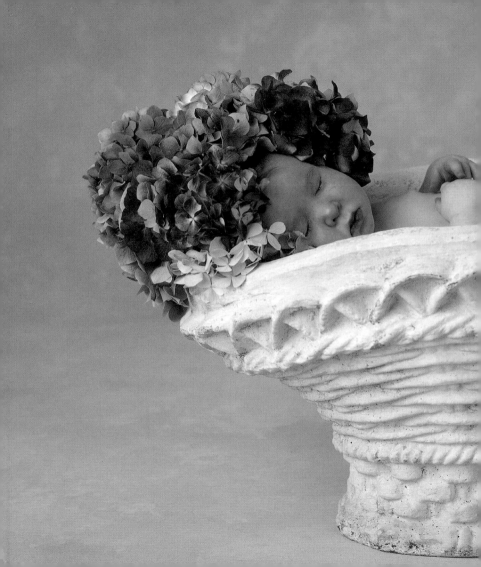

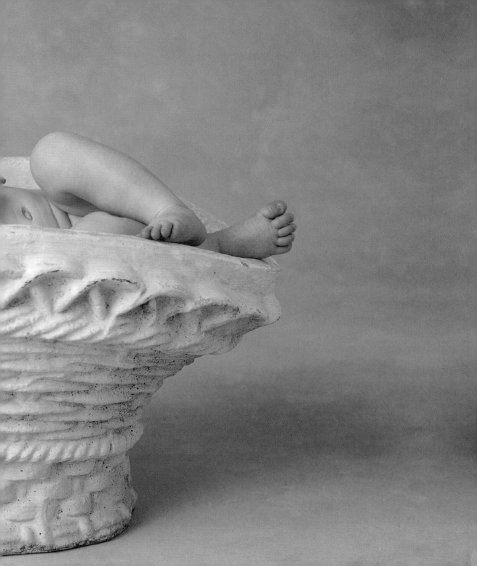

Sometimes
the BEST
flowers arrive
unexpectedly.

Previous Page: Monica   Opposite: Christopher

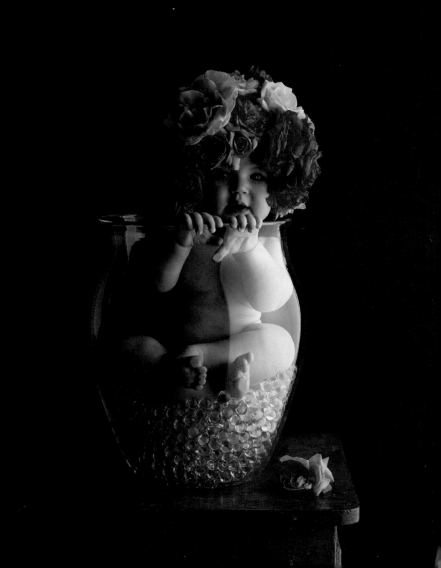

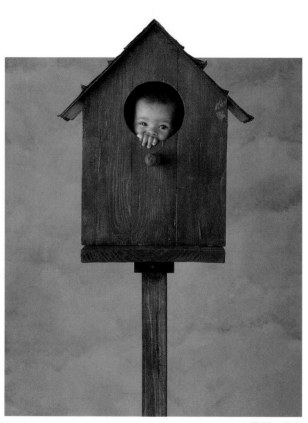

Fledgling: Kayla

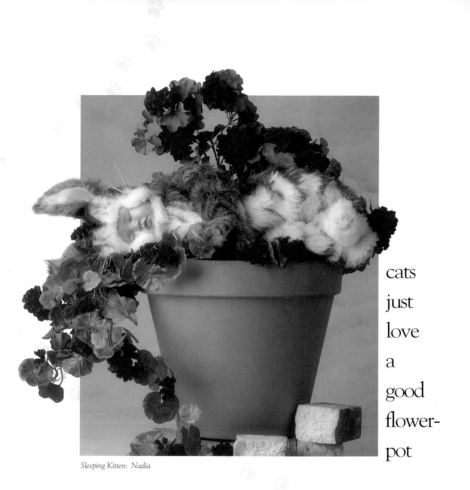

cats
just
love
a
good
flower-
pot

Sleeping Kitten: Nadia

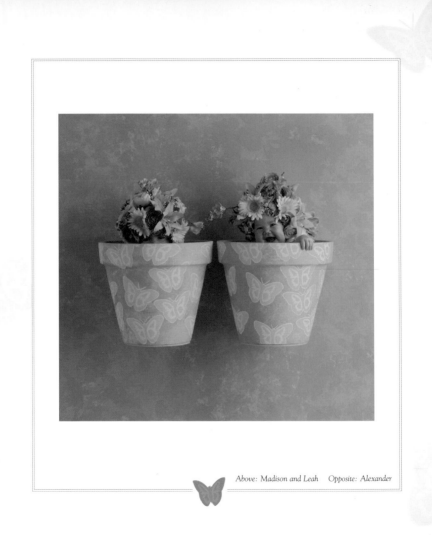

Above: Madison and Leah   Opposite: Alexander

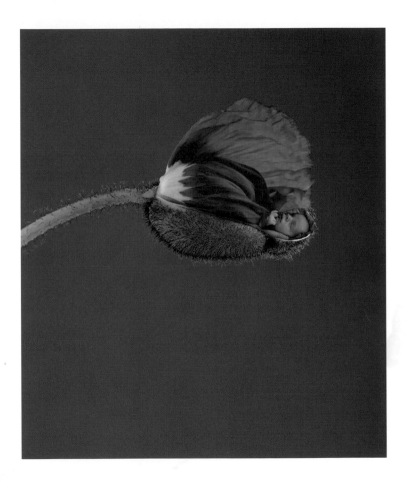

Remember

when

you were

small

and you

thought

pansies

had

faces.

(L–R): Aisha, Tayla and Grace

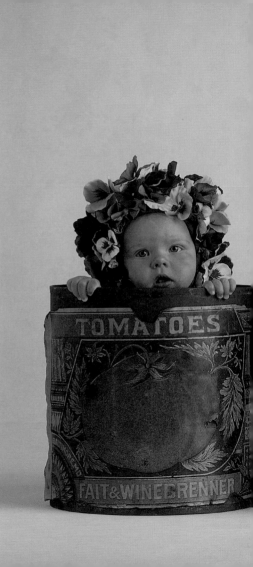

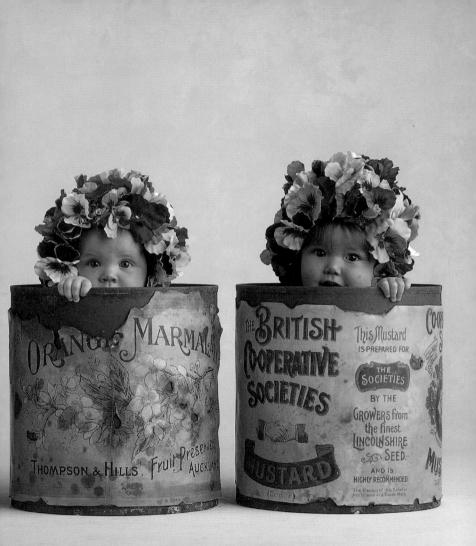

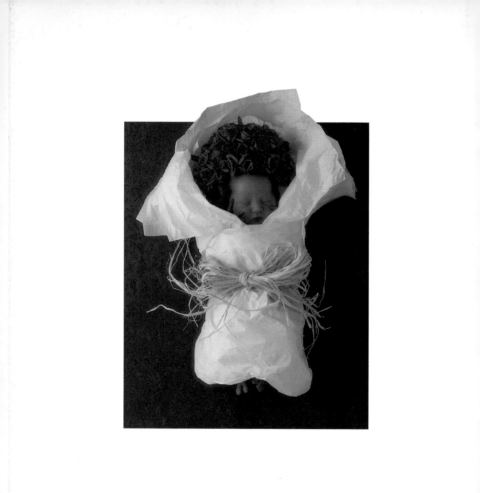

Apricot Bouquet: Danielle   Wet Sparrow: Tyla

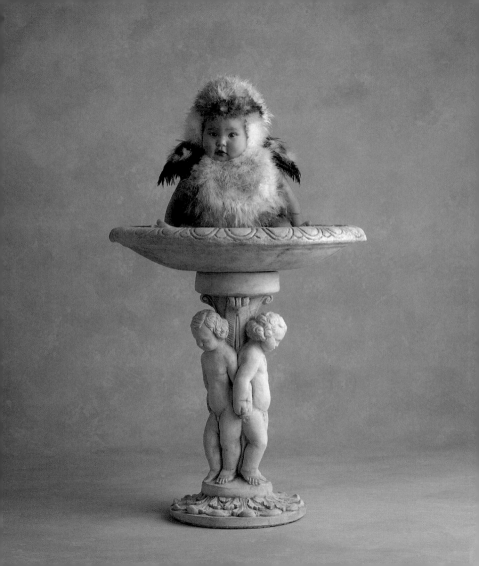

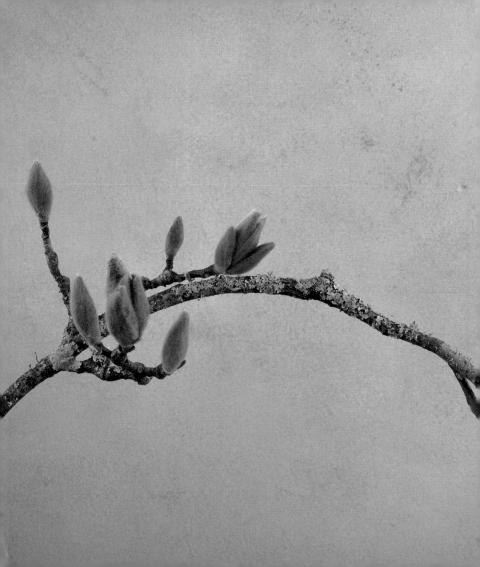

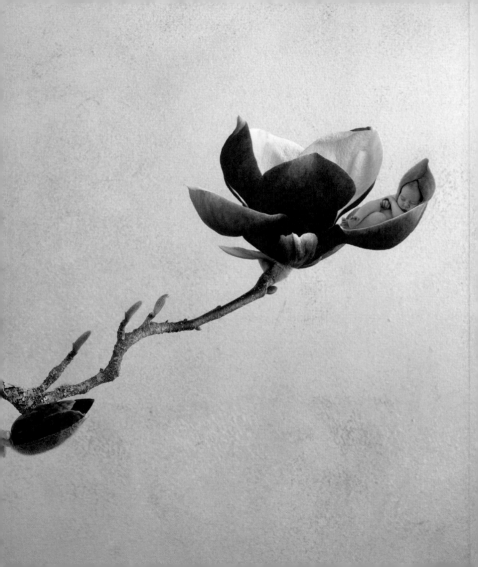

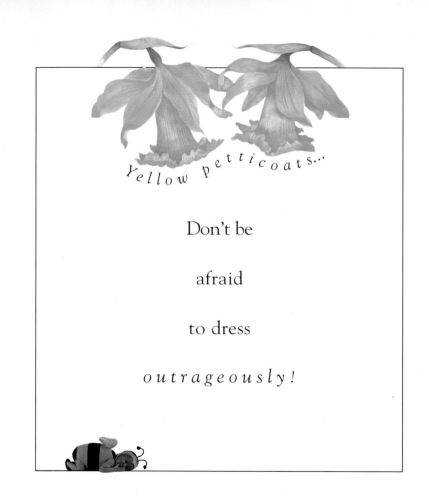

Yellow petticoats...

Don't be

afraid

to dress

outrageously!

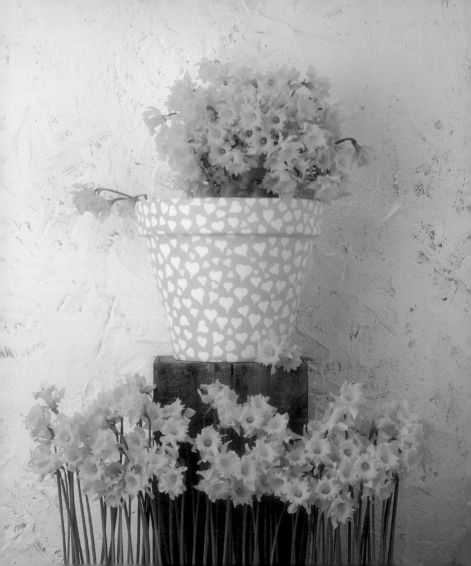

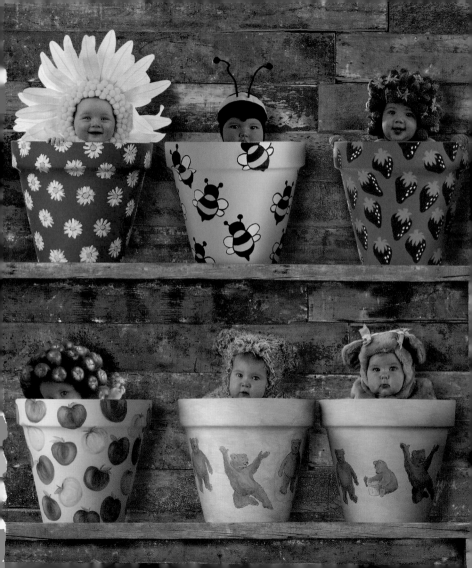

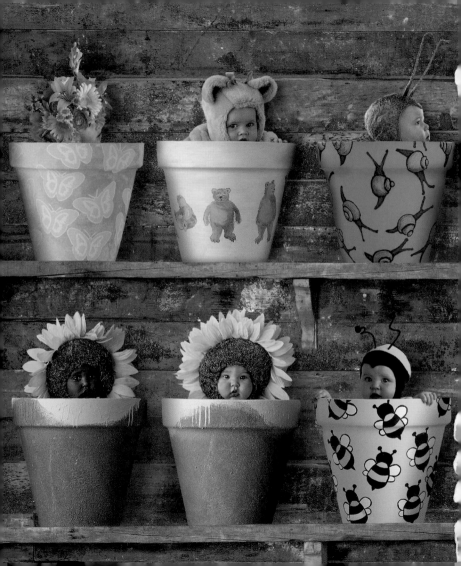

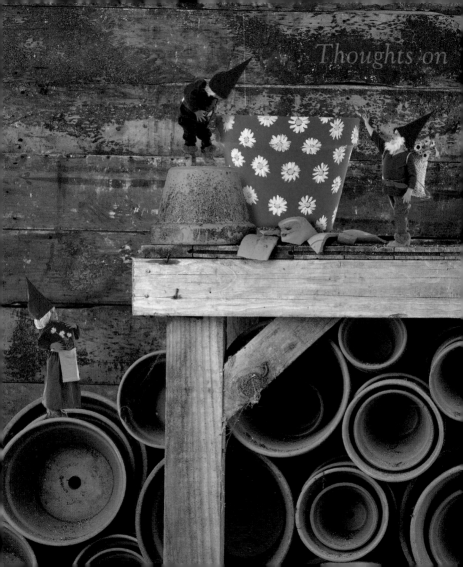

Thoughts on

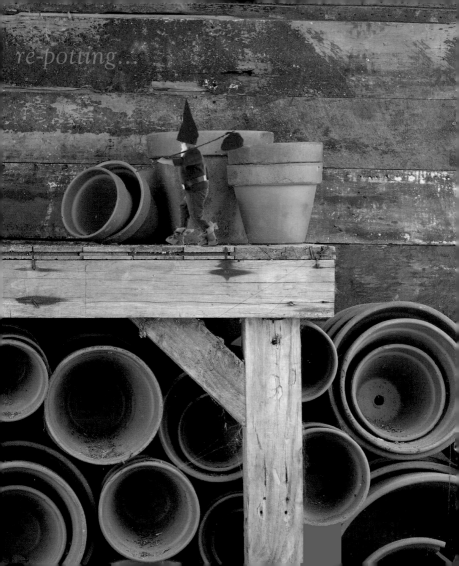

re-potting...

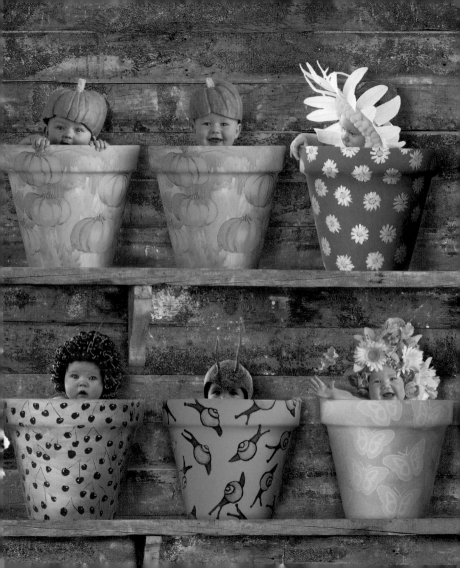

Don't forget to

s e p a r a t e

your bulbs before

they become too crowded.

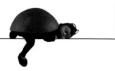

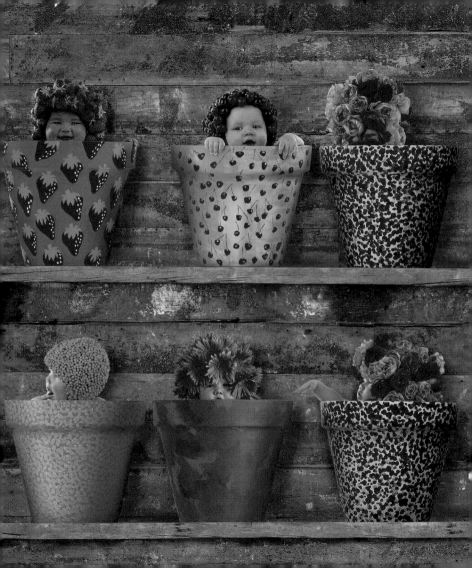

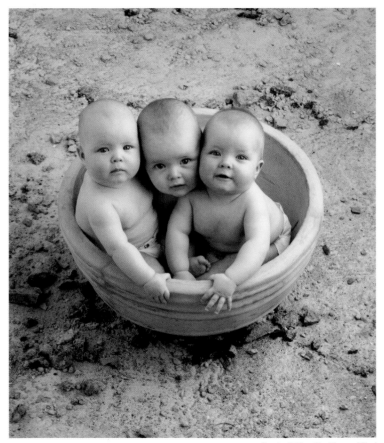

Starring Triplets: Jim, Flora and Pearl

Have your goldfish been disappearing lately?

Remember to keep your lily pond well-stocked...

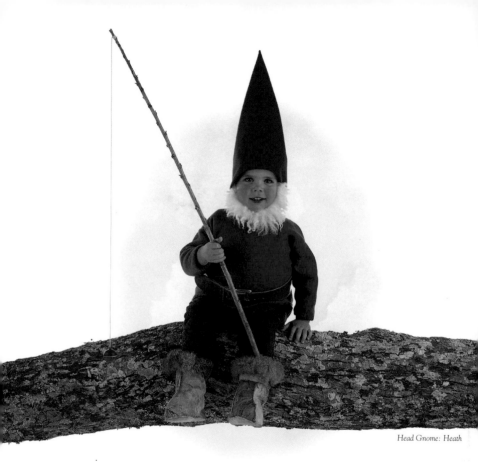

Head Gnome: Heath

Waterlily: Tayla

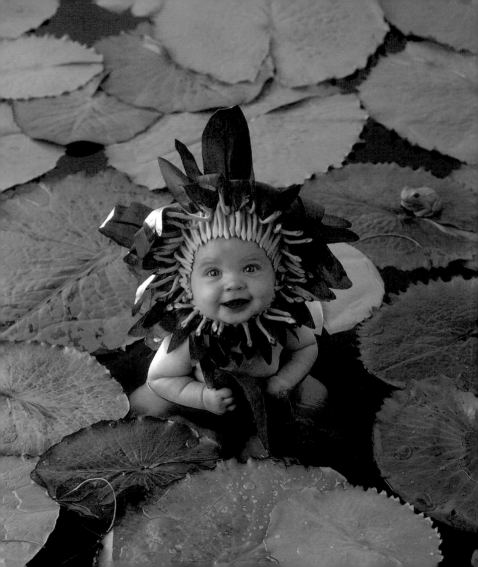

And you thought

babies ONLY

came from under

cabbage leaves.

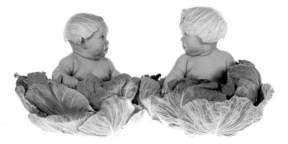

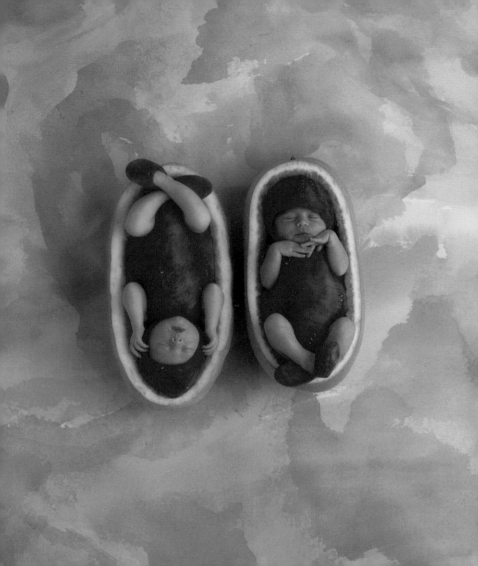

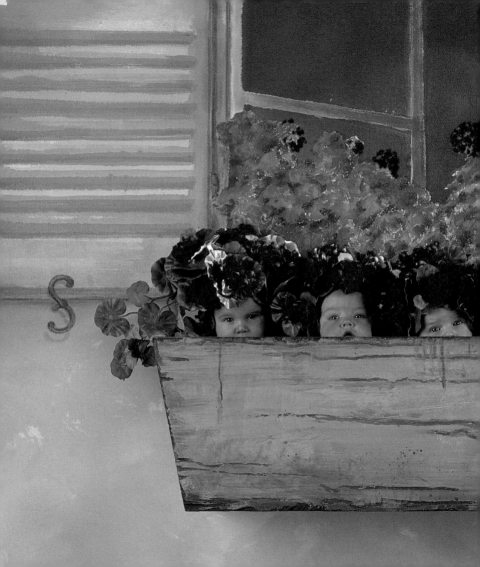

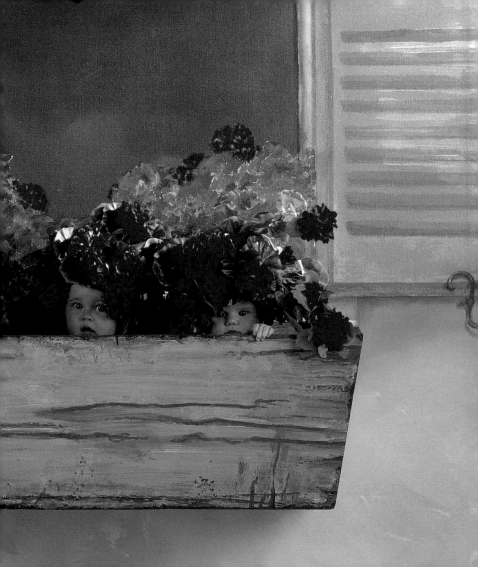

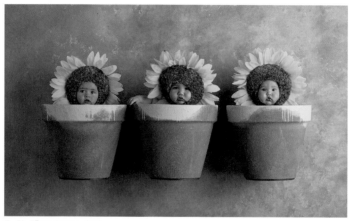

(L–R): Ellecia, Jayson and Tyla

I like Sunflowers

they make me feel happy

by stacey
aged 6

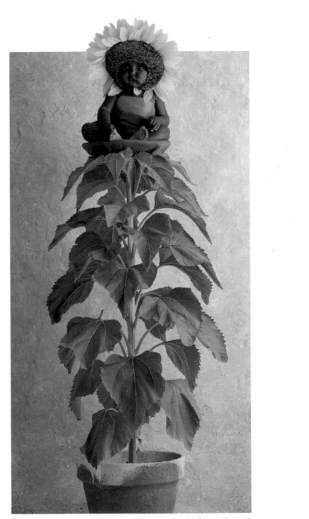

Sunflower: Henneock

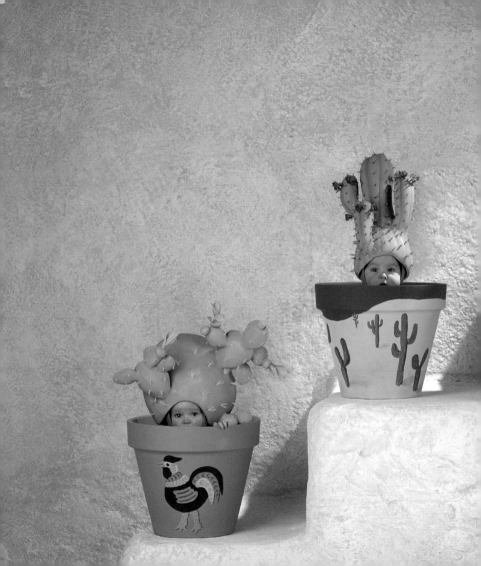

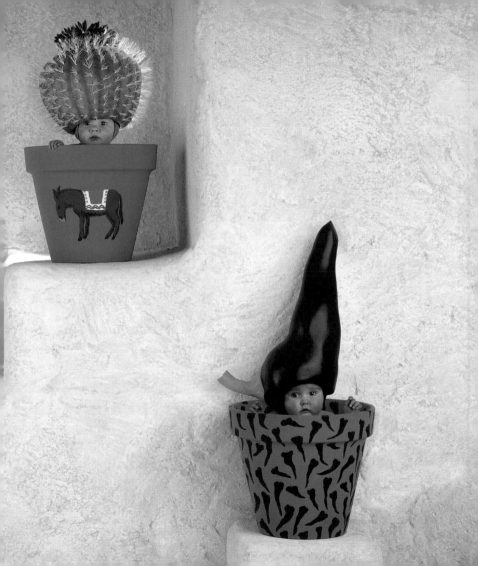

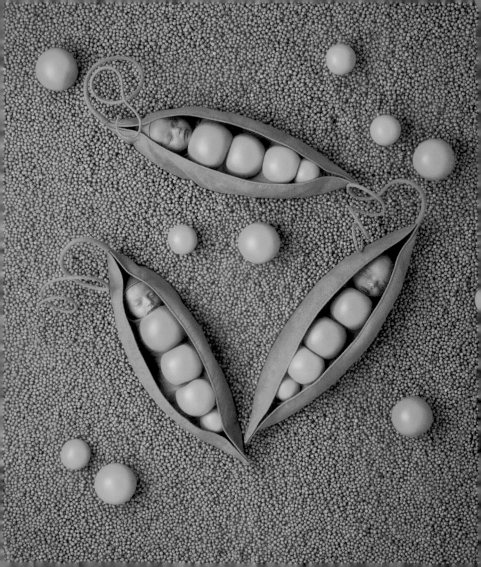

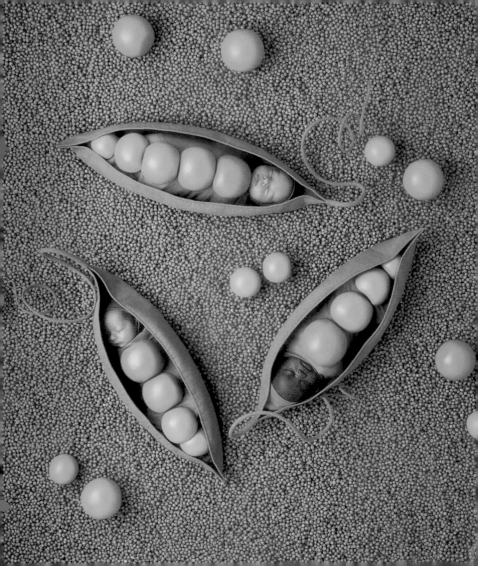

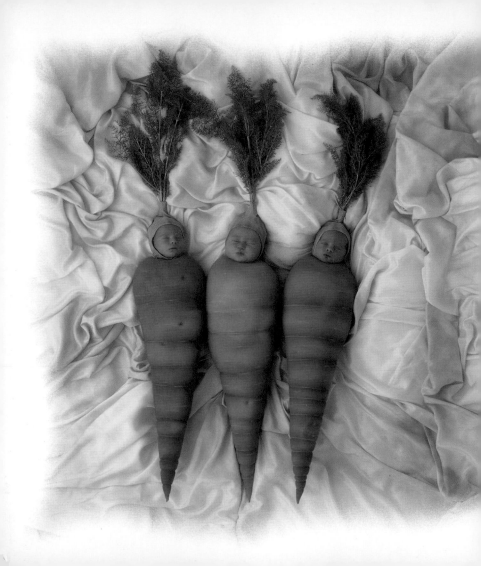

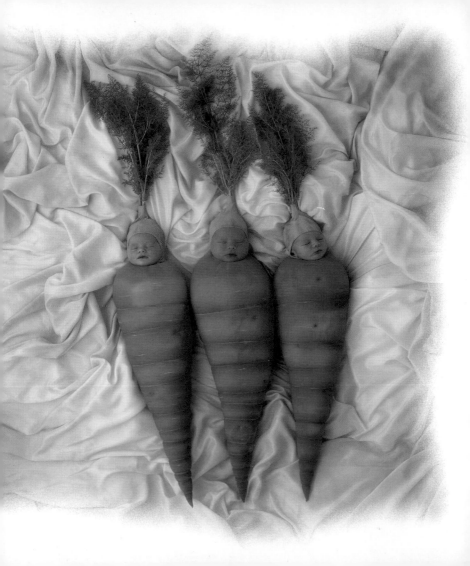

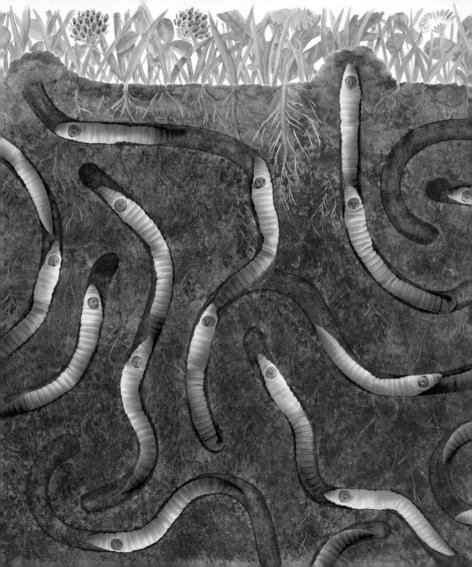

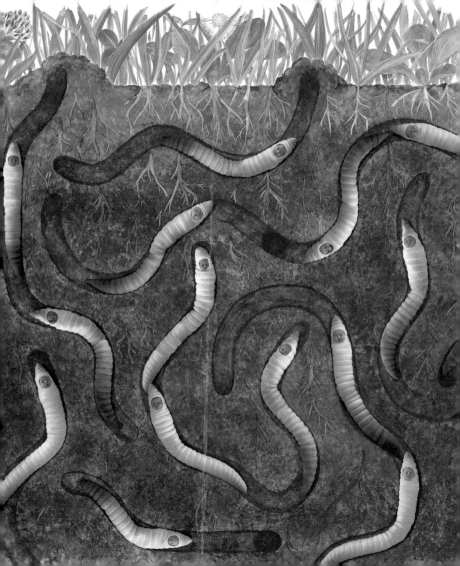

"There is no living being more *humble* than the earthworm." Charles Darwin was moved to write that "of all animals, few have contributed so much to the development of the world, as we know it, as earthworms." [*1]

Bringing their own unique charm to *"Peggy's Worm Farm,"* are 55 little newborn babies (no one worm repeated), who were photographed over a period of 6 months.

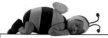

"I once heard that bumblebees

don't have their own homes, but they

love sleeping *inside* pumpkin flowers.

Sometimes when it's cloudy, the flowers

close *early*..."

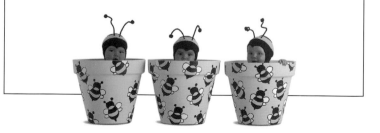

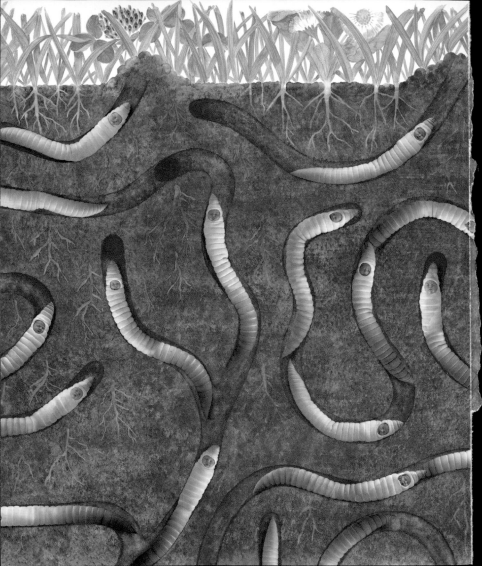

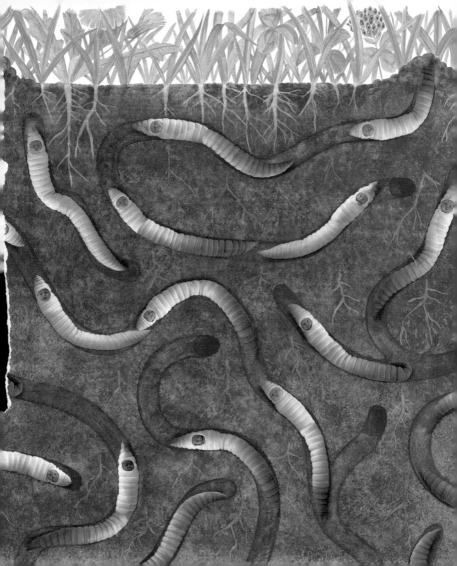

The inhabitants are:

Courtney, Hayley, Samuel, Benjamin, Alexander, Liam, Cara, Tyrone, Emma, Hayley, Jaimee, Danielle, Bryce, Joshua, Danielle, Alexander, Harry, Jasmine, Elijah, Taylor, Maxine, Kasey, Lucy, Georgia, Te Naawe, Khan, Kayleen, Laura, Asher, Whitney, Adelia, Nicholas, Rebecca, Beaudene, Mitchell, Taylor, Daniel, Caitlin, Alec, Natasha, Jessie, Tara, Grace, Gene, Hannah, Michaela, Marni, Holly, Elise, Thomas, Charlotte, Nana Yaw, Dennison, Jessica and Rebekah.

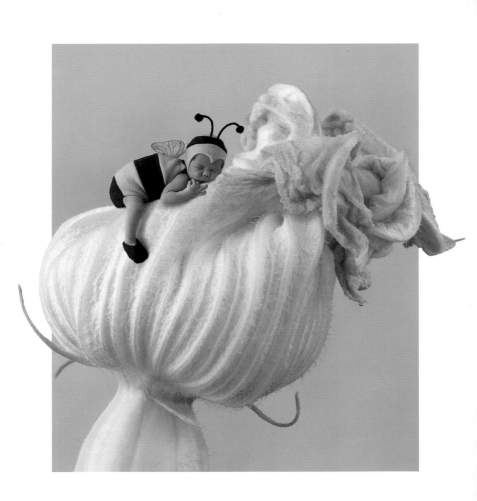

A
clucky
hen

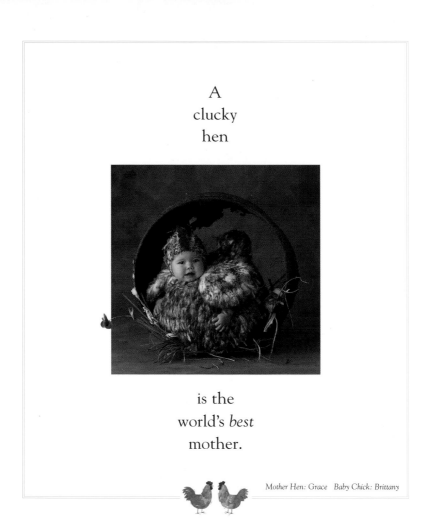

is the
world's *best*
mother.

Mother Hen: Grace   Baby Chick: Brittany

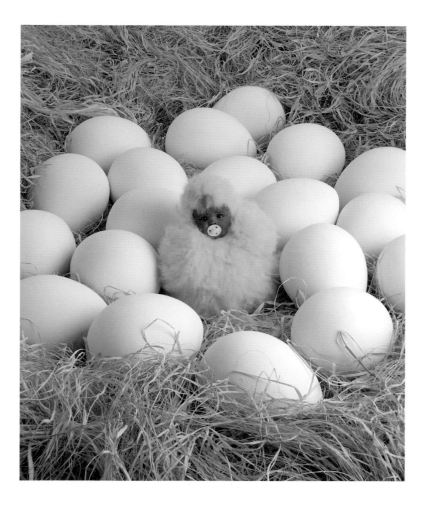

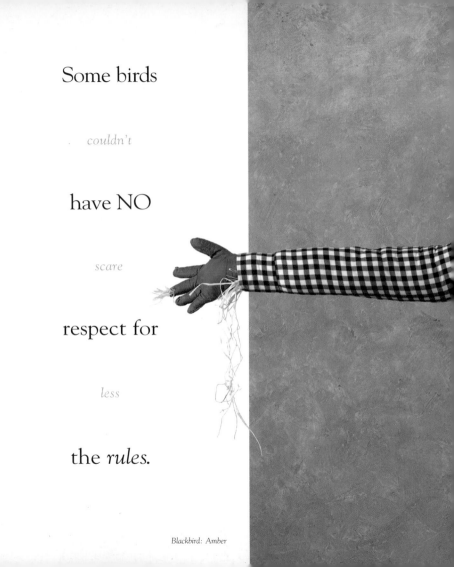

Some birds

couldn't

have NO

scare

respect for

less

the *rules.*

Blackbird: Amber

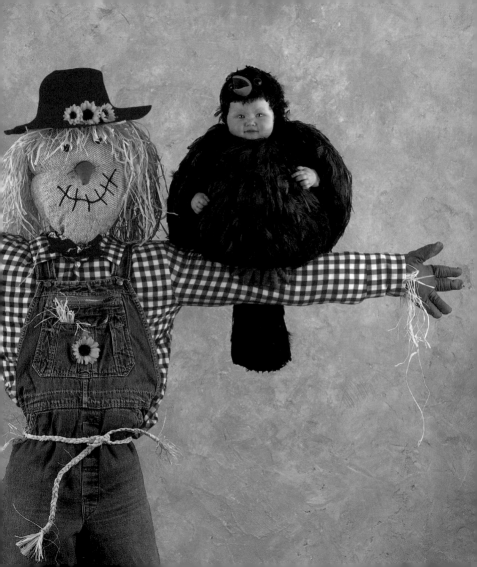

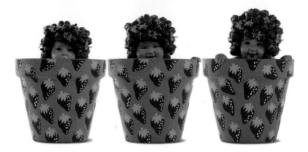

Home·grown

strawberries

The

cream

of the

crop.

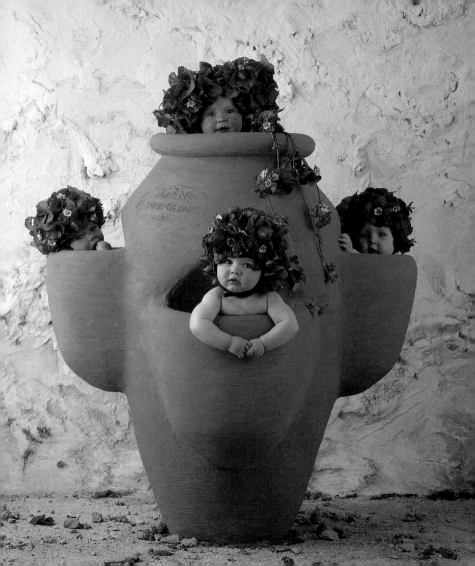

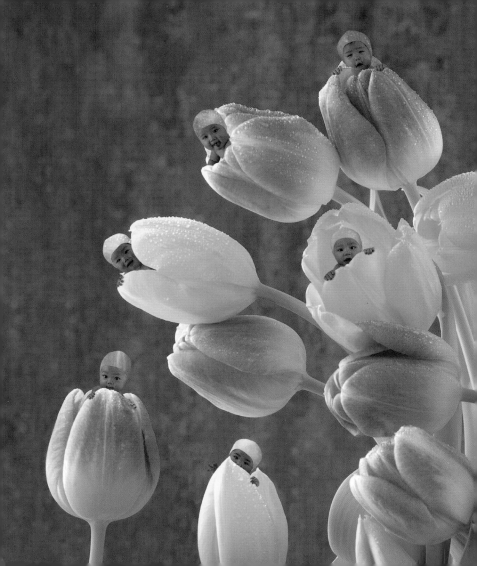

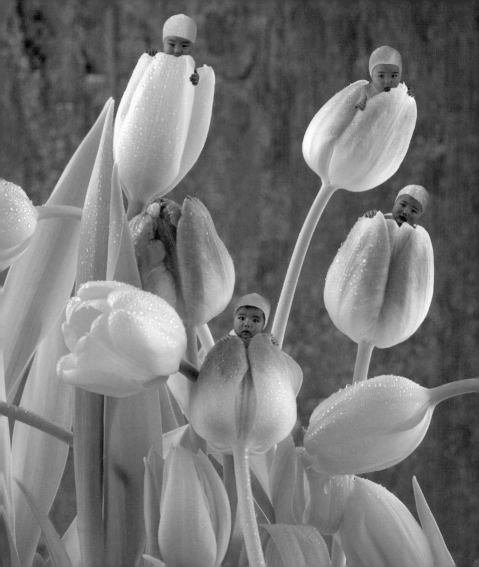

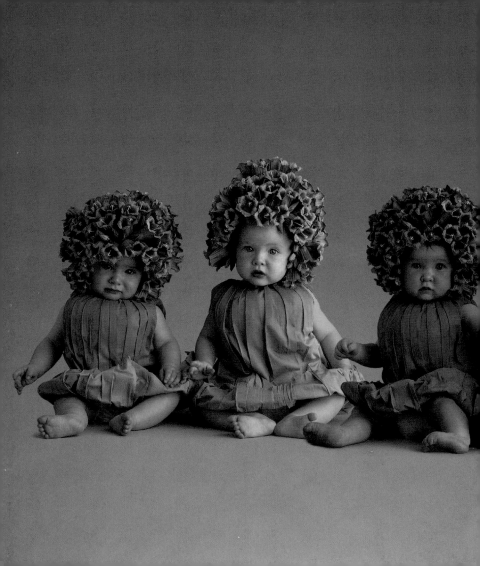

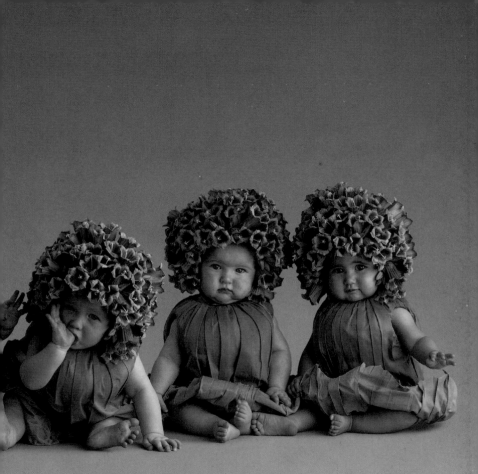

Canterbury Belles

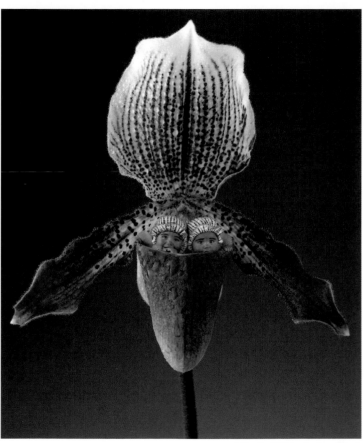

Slipper Orchid Twins: Brooke and Starcia

Hydrangiss Babyiss
(Rare Bloom)

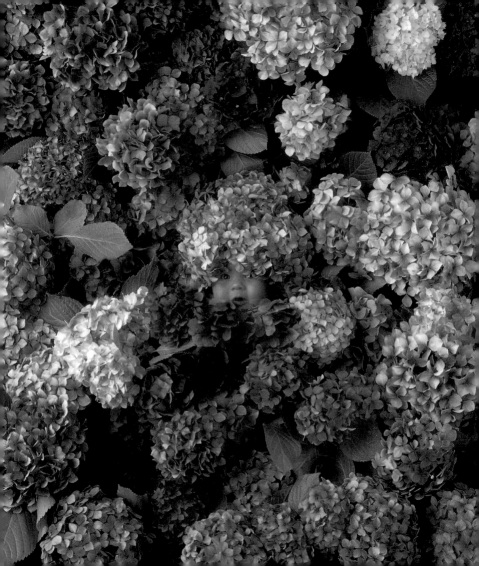

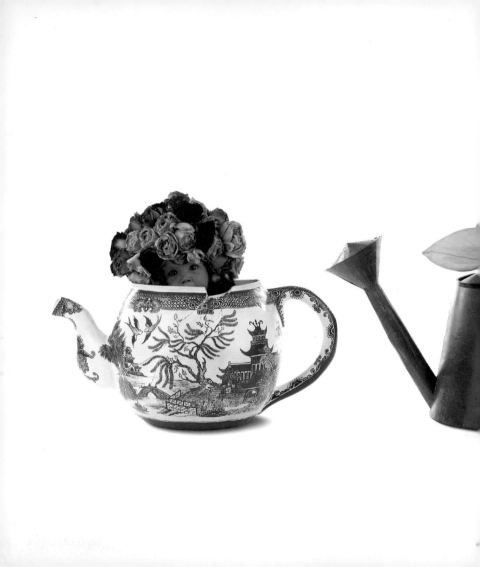

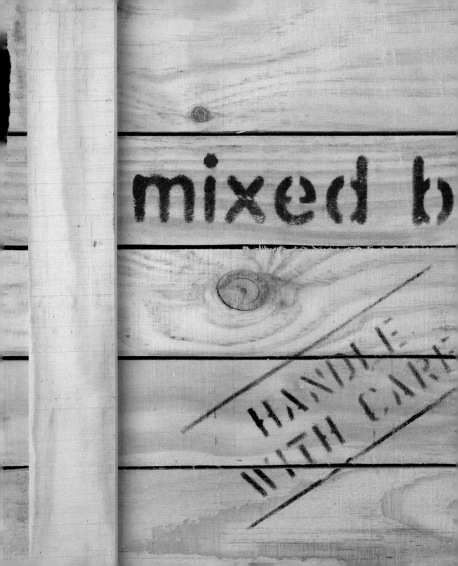

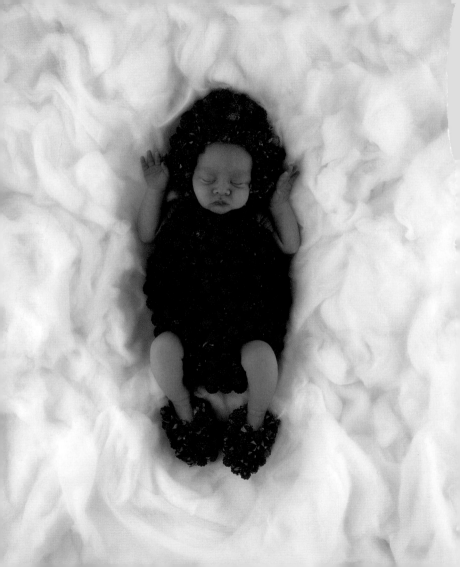

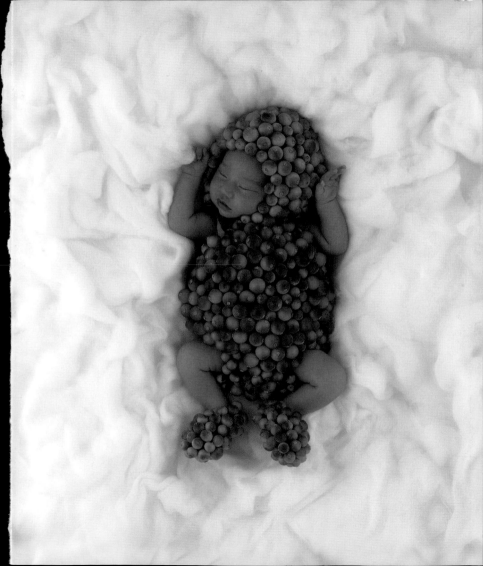

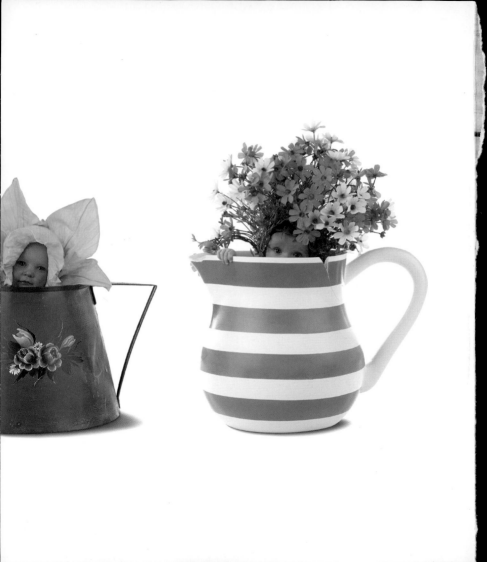

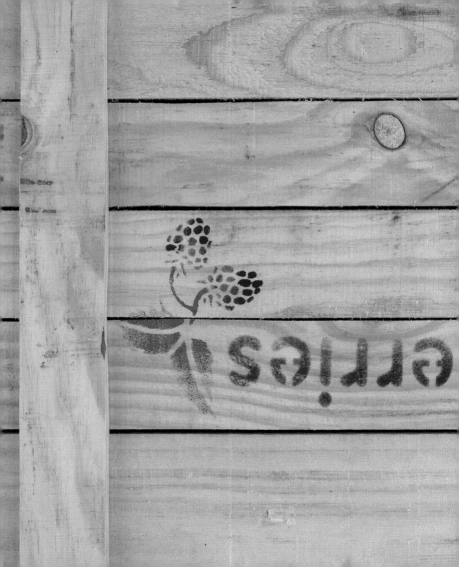

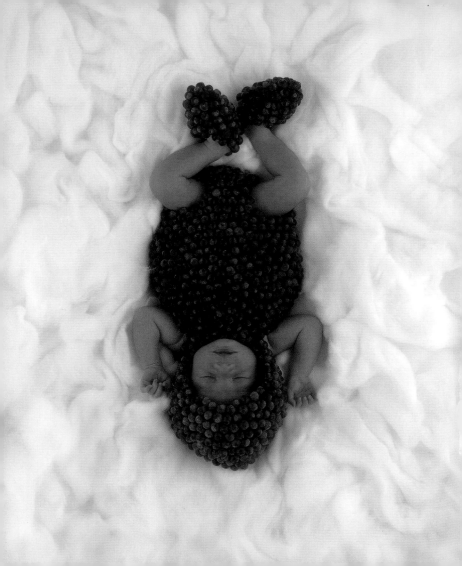

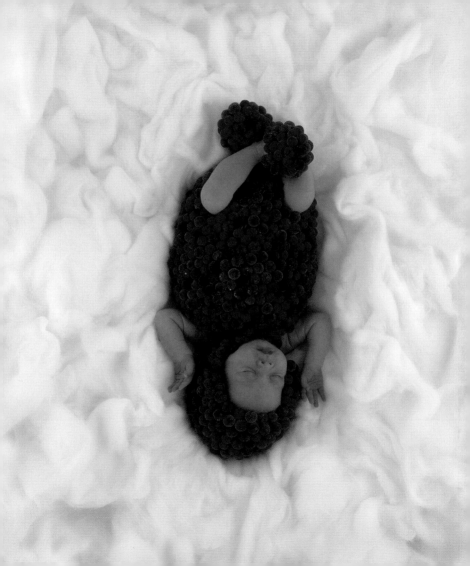

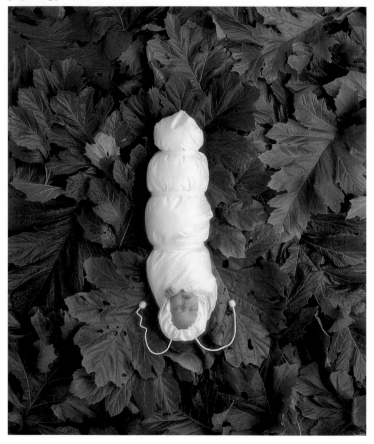

The

Ultimate

Makeover...

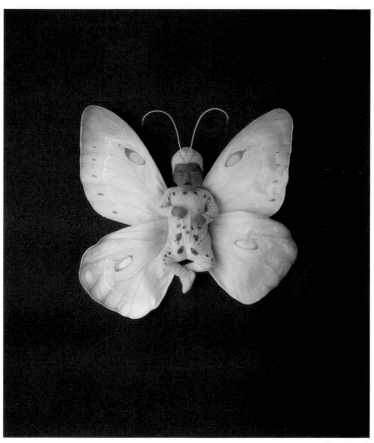

Fiona Butterfly

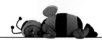

Gardening Terms of Endearment

♥

Sweet Pea

Blossom

Rosebud

Petal

Pumpkin

Honeybunch

♥

*Never miss an opportunity
to tell someone you love them.*

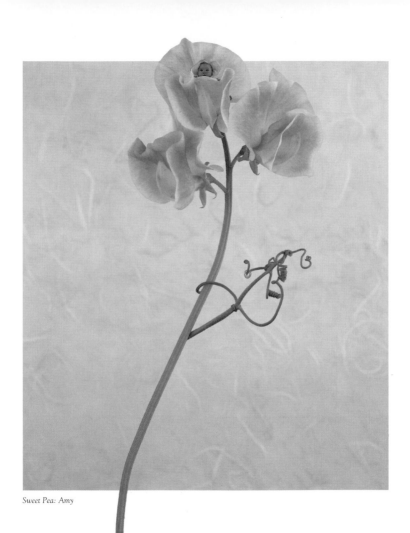

Sweet Pea: Amy

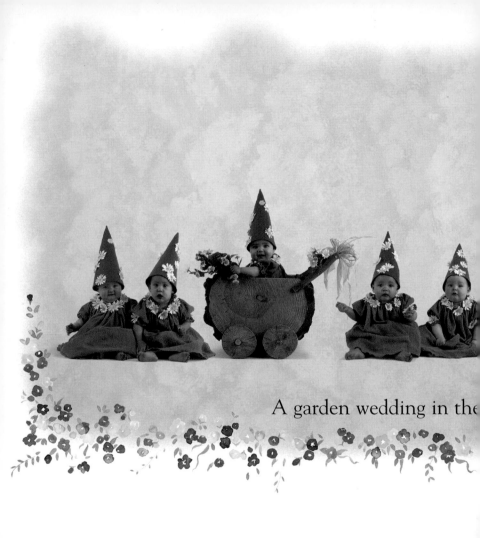

A garden wedding in the

Summertime is always delightful.

Until

recently

it was

thought that

gnome mothers

only ever

had *twins*.

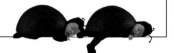

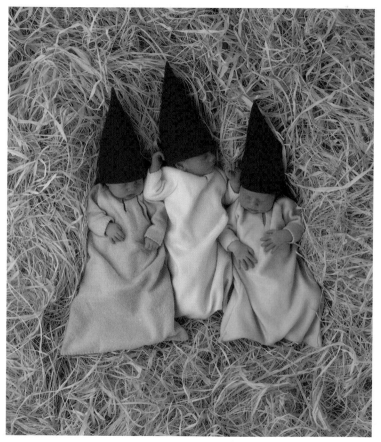

Newborn Gnomes: Laura, Te Naawe and Kayleen

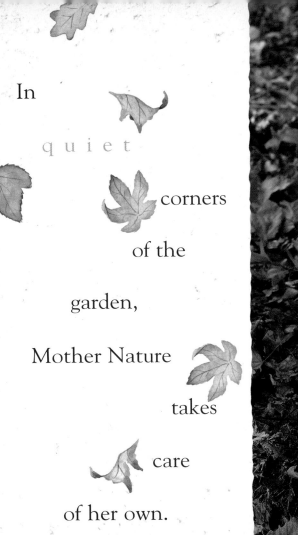

In

quiet

corners

of the

garden,

Mother Nature

takes

care

of her own.

Woodland Fairy: Sophie

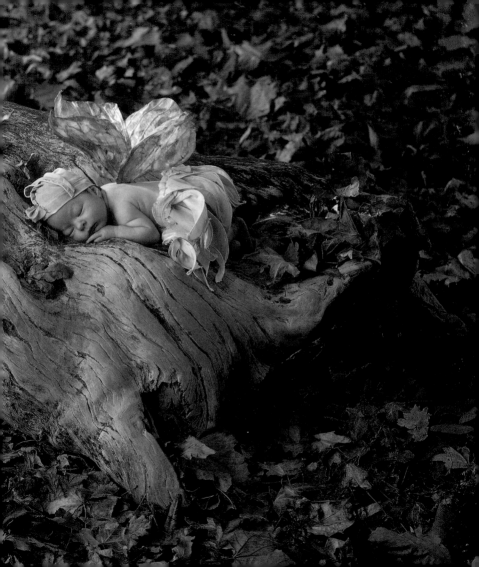

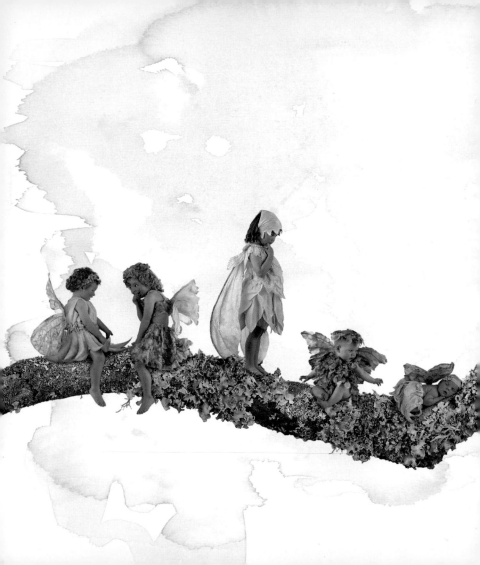

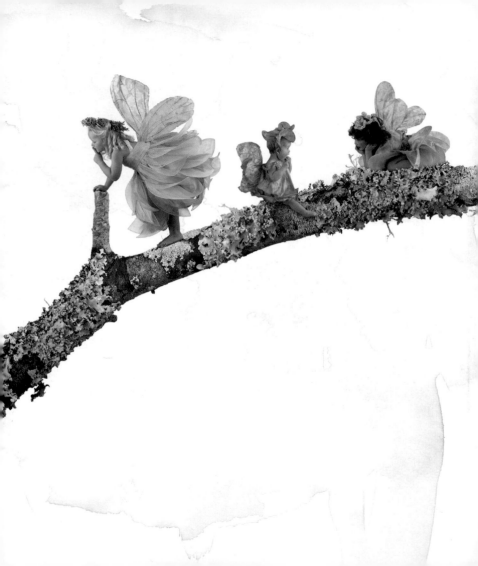

In the Autumn

you can look

forward to

unexpected

overnight

visitors...

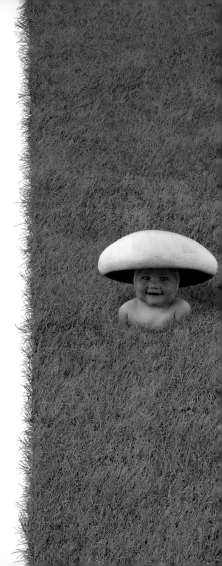

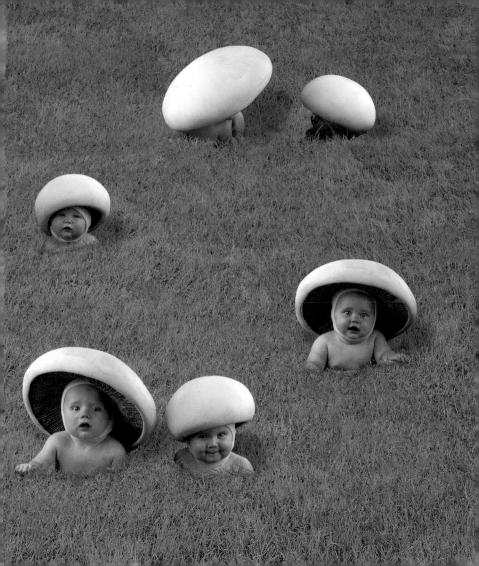

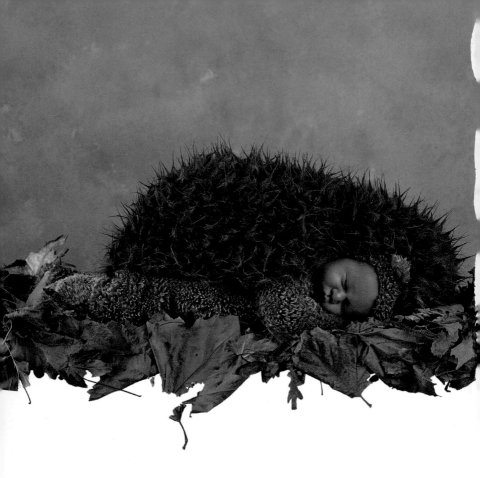

Every now and then, leave out a saucer of milk for the hedgehogs.

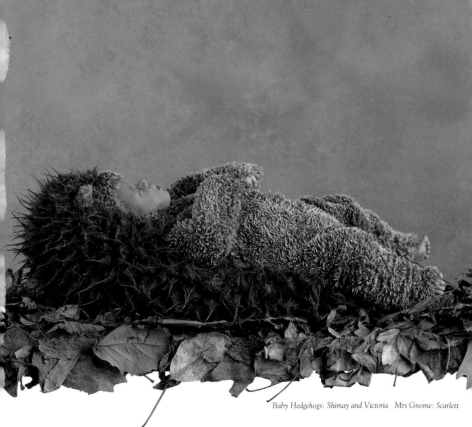

Baby Hedgehogs: Shimay and Victoria   Mrs Gnome: Scarlett

It keeps them out of the hen house.

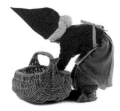

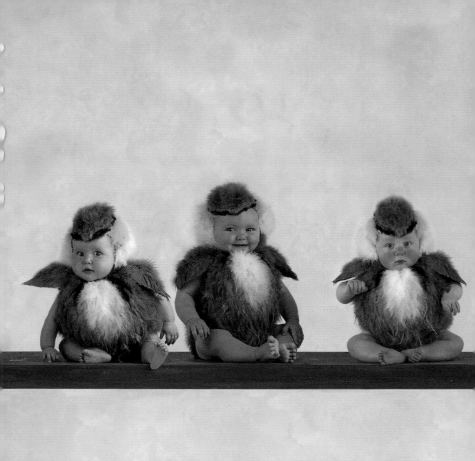

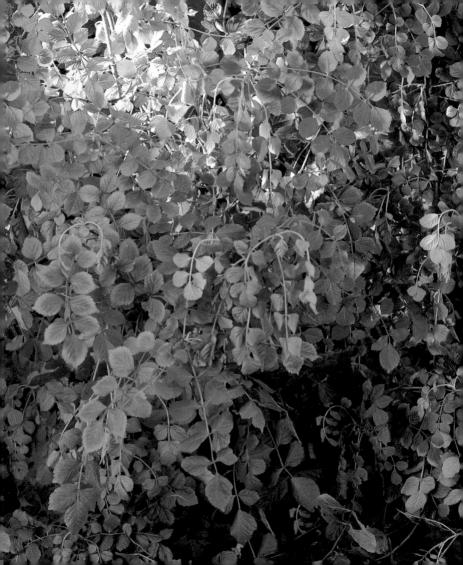

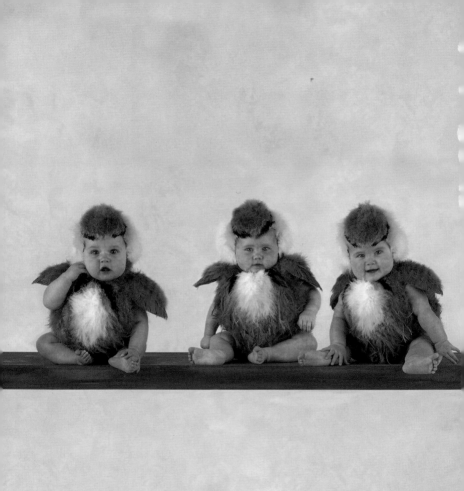

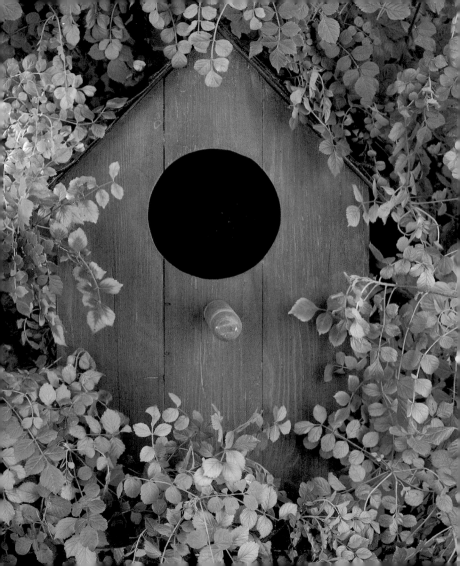

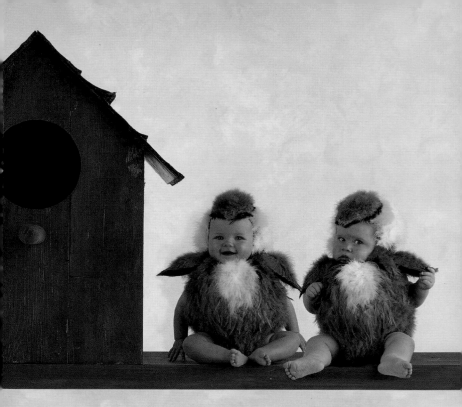

You're never without friends,

when you have a birdhouse in your garden.

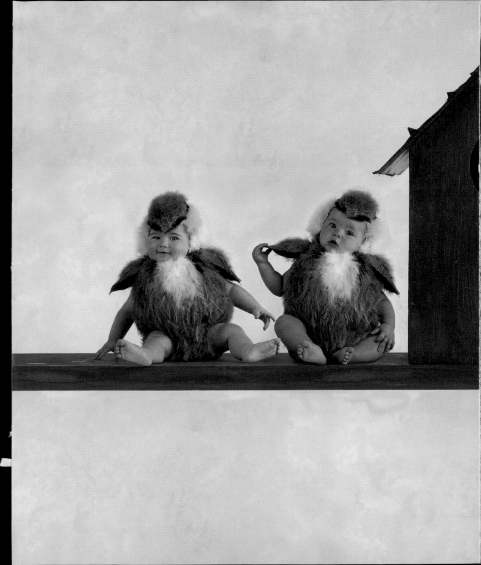

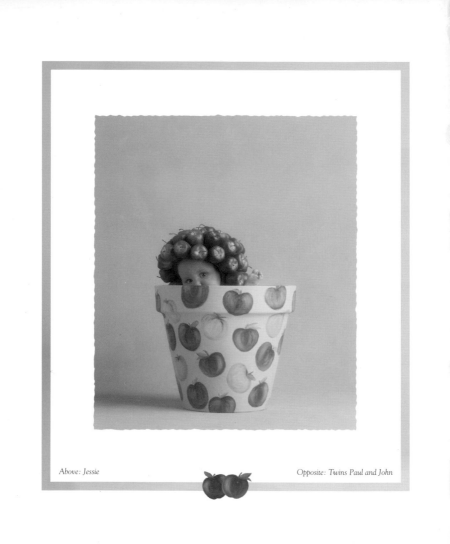

Above: Jessie

Opposite: Twins Paul and John

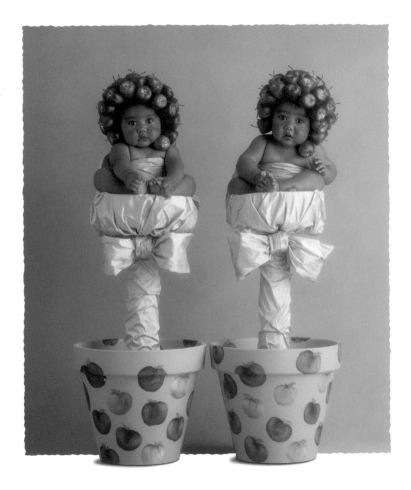

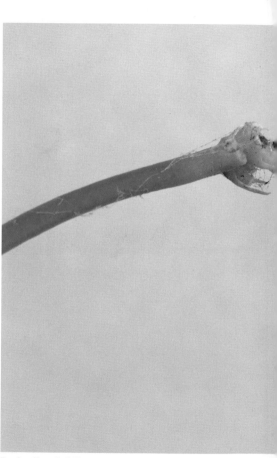

Parachute Flower Bud: Elise

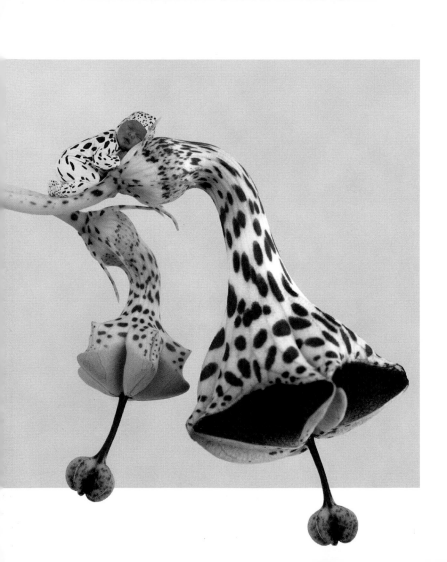

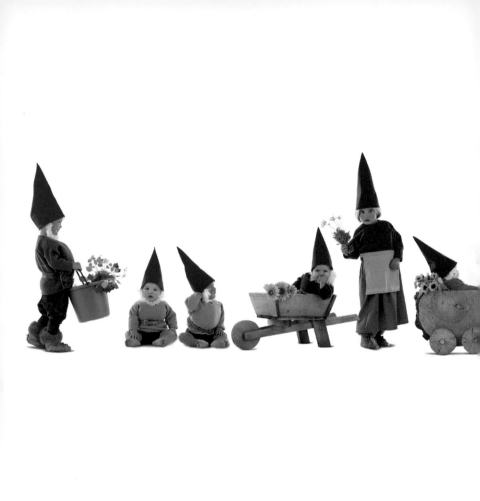

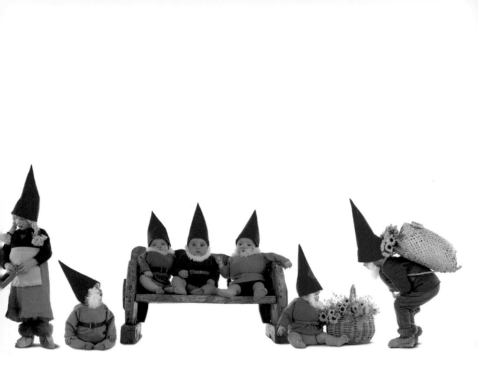

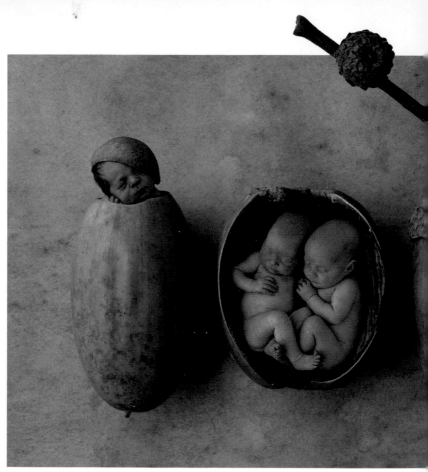

Two sets of Twins: Evan and Dean (together); Thomas and Elizabeth

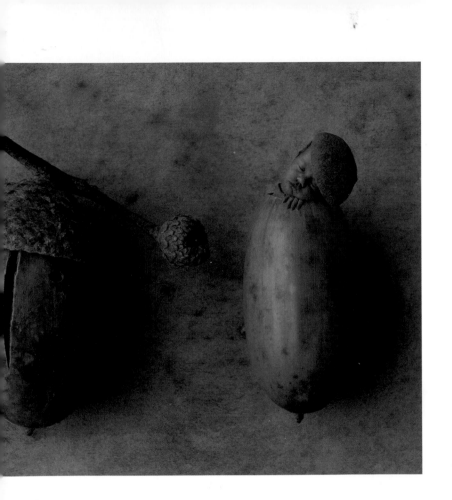

Be careful not to tread on acorns in the Autumn.

When
stocking
up for Winter,
remember to gather
enough for a friend.

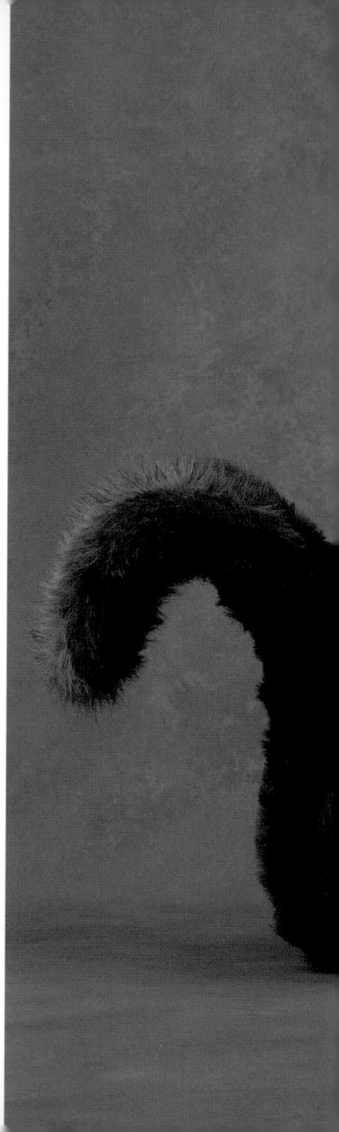

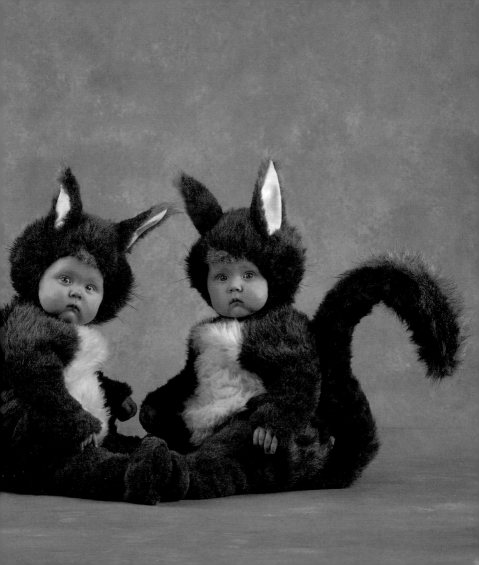

All *kinds* of babies

grow well in gardens.

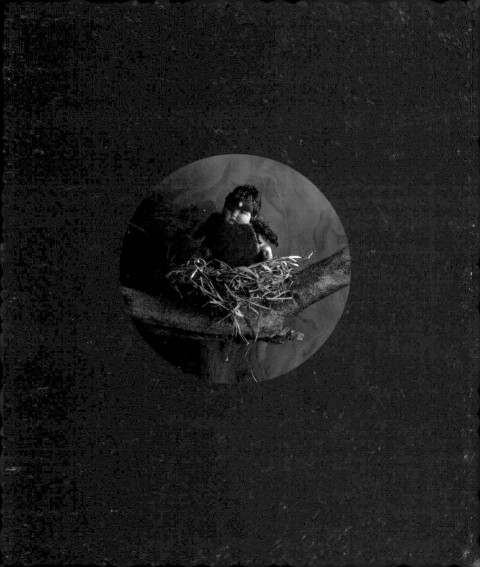

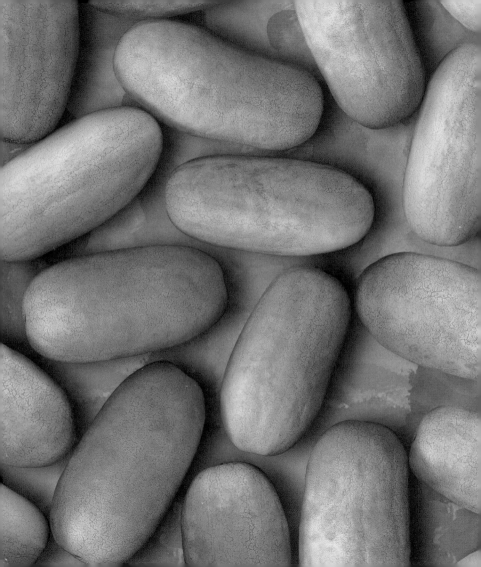

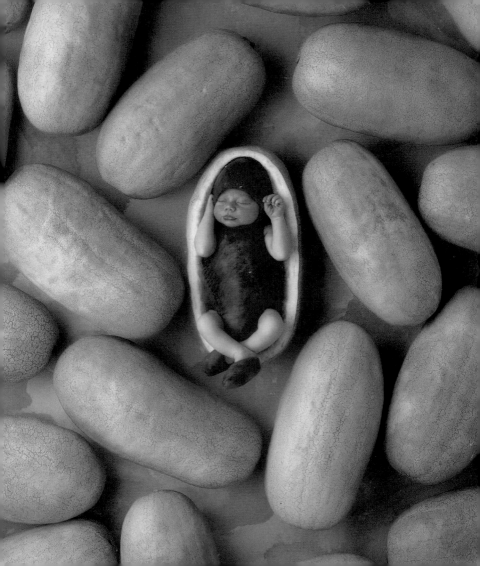

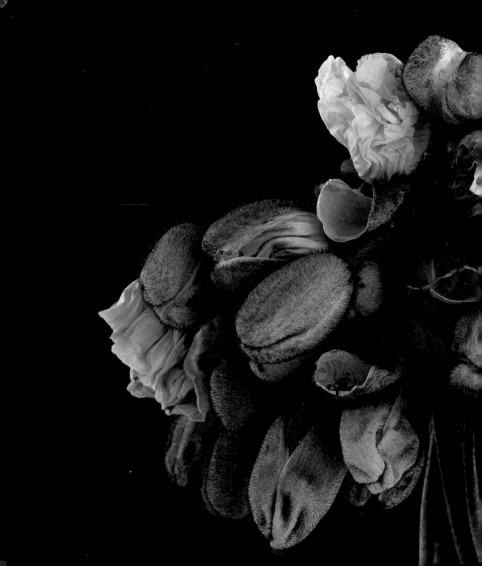

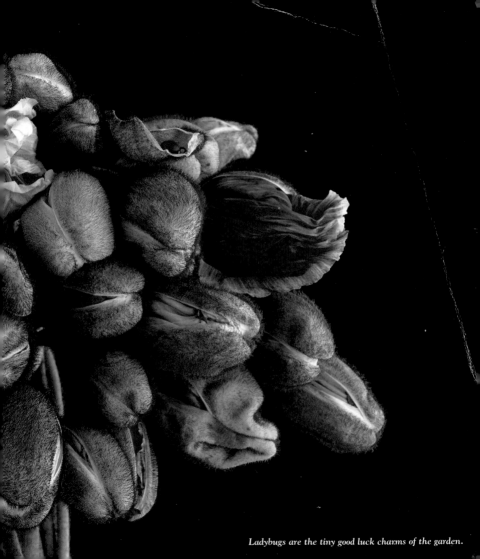

Ladybugs are the tiny good luck charms of the garden.

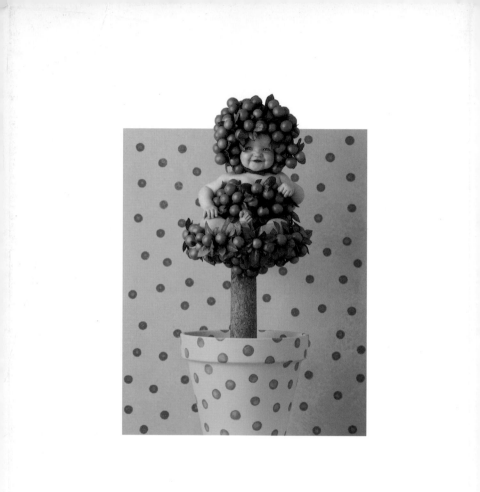

Above: Shani Facing Page (L-R): Shani, Joshua and Cole

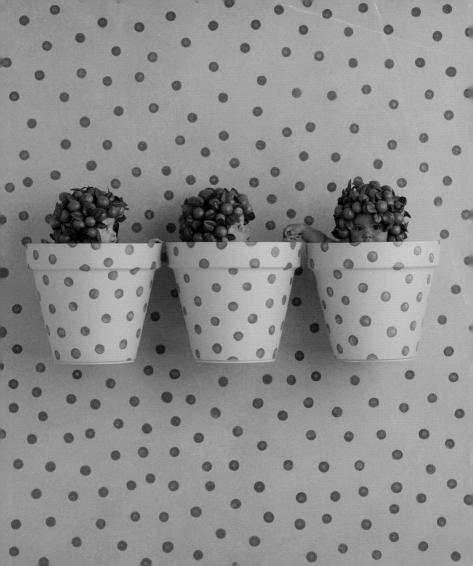

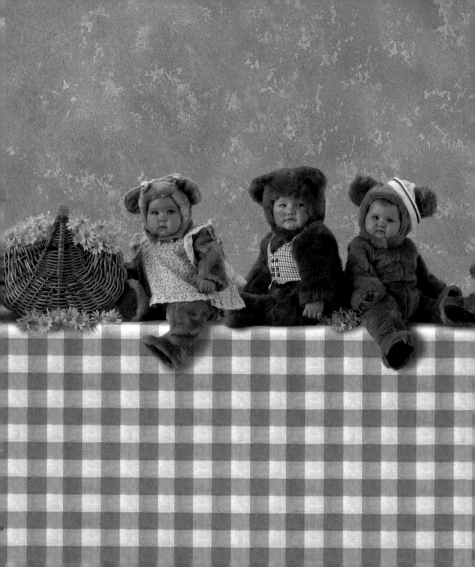

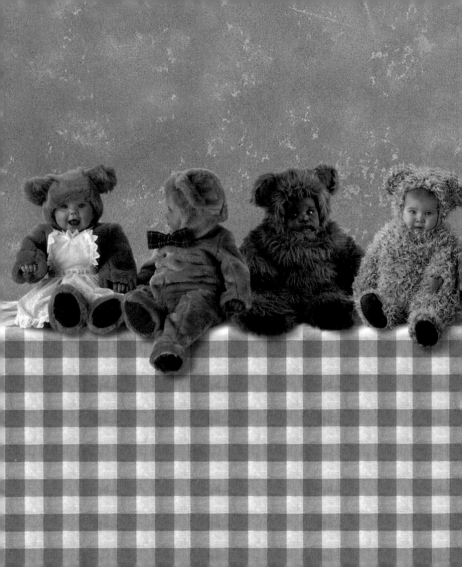

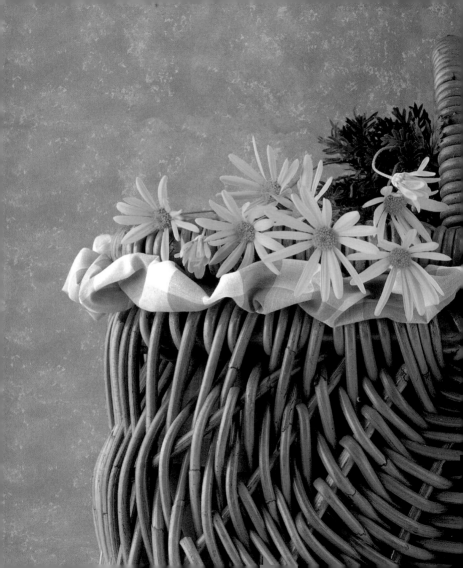

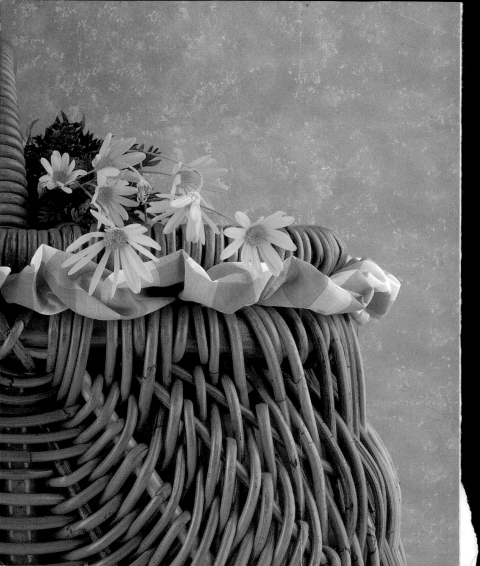

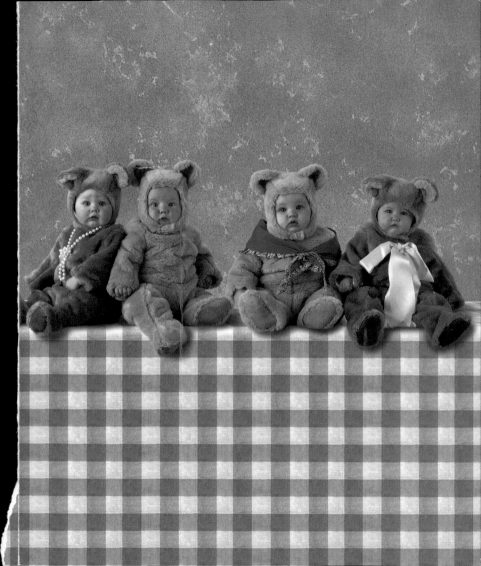

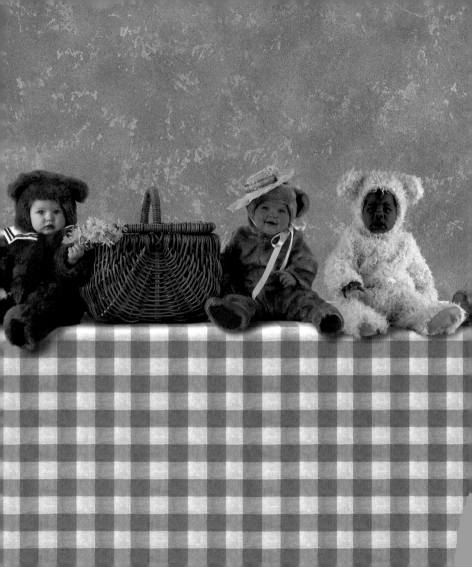

Pool Party

Fun

is

where

you

find it.

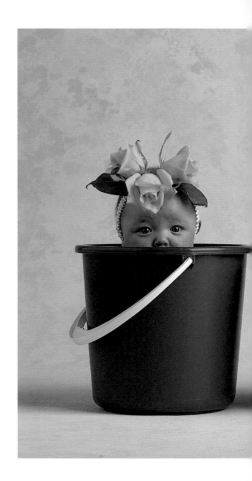

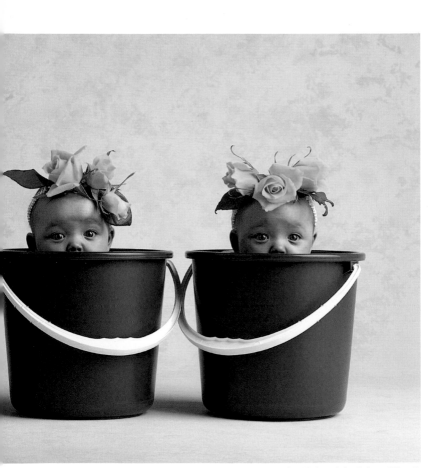

Backyard Bathers, Triplets: Alesha, Kailee, and Chantelle

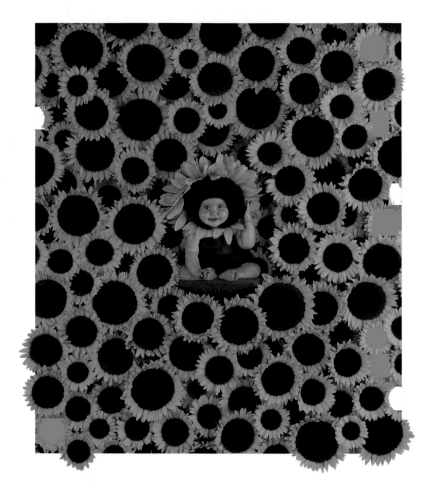

Sunflower: Alexandra   Sunflower Centers: Twins, Rahul and Alvina

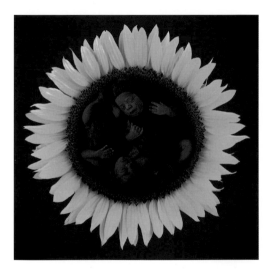

"Time makes roses."

Proverb

Devote

the

time....

Adam

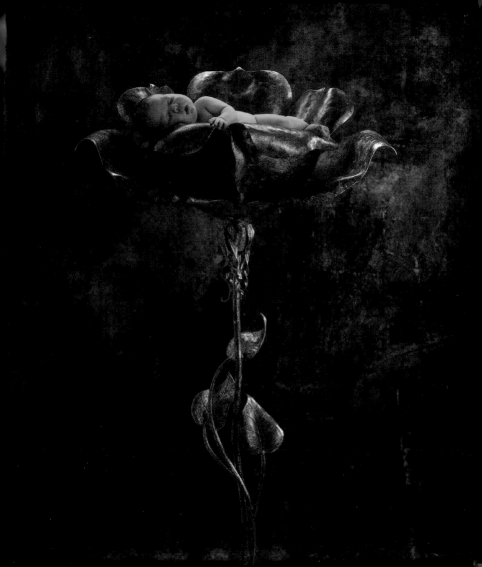

Cast of Characters